Diary of an
APPRENTICE

Book One in the Series
Diaries of a Shaman

Diary of an APPRENTICE

Book One in the Series
Diaries of a Shaman

By
DreamSnake

BALBOA.
PRESS
A DIVISION OF HAY HOUSE

The views expressed in this work are solely those of the author and do not necessarily reflect the views of the publisher, and the publisher hereby disclaims any responsibility for them.

Balboa Press books may be ordered through booksellers or by contacting:

Balboa Press
A Division of Hay House
1663 Liberty Drive
Bloomington, IN 47403
www.balboapress.com.au

1-(877) 407-4847
ISBN: 978-1-4525-0678-4 (sc)
ISBN: 978-1-4525-0677-7 (e)

Because of the dynamic nature of the Internet, any web addresses or links contained in this book may have changed since publication and may no longer be valid.

The author of this book does not dispense medical advice or prescribe the use of any technique as a form of treatment for physical, emotional, or medical problems without the advice of a physician, either directly or indirectly. The intent of the author is only to offer information of a general nature to help you in your quest for emotional and spiritual well-being. In the event you use any of the information in this book for yourself, which is your constitutional right, the author and the publisher assume no responsibility for your actions.

Cover Design by Alan Davidson

Printed in the United States of America

CONTENTS

Foreword

I am asked to review quite a number of books that relate to a mystical or metaphysical nature. With most of them I am happy to oblige. I refuse a few for various reasons, but seldom do I resonate to a manuscript in the way that I have with *Diary of an Apprentice*. This is rather like reading the stories of myself at an earlier stage of my journey, but, of course, they are also very different. These reflect the uniqueness of the author, recounting his many journeys and experiences in – what I call – a Greater reality. There are not many people who learn to cross the membrane between the visible, tangible world into the invisible, non-tangible world, yet the author has accomplished this brilliantly.

His journey stories will take you from physical and non-physical aborigines in the bush, to lines and balls of light, and on to the distant stars, yet all have one thing in common: authenticity. It is only when you have made similar journeys that you know the authenticity of another person's account.

This is an excellent book; I suggest you read it slowly. This allows the author's journey to reach to a deeper level within, opening the reader to the vast unknown in which we live.

MICHAEL J. ROADS

Author of the best selling classics:
Talking with Nature and *Journey into Nature*

And his recent;
Through the Eyes of Love - Journeying with Pan
www.michaelroads.com

Introduction

The Air Chakra

I fled upwards, ridding myself of the fear and hatred that swept through the earth, infecting the minds and bodies of the people, and breaking against my aura like a continuous wave. From afar, I looked down upon this planet of blues and greens, delicately swirled in white. It was truly beautiful.

Red fissures opened, running through the earth, cutting across the greens and blues – the lines of war – separating the people. I flared, and in a great anger loosed bolts of energy from my fingertips to rid the earth of this despair.

Surprised by my anger, I withdrew … backtracking through the lines of energy until I stood above the earth as before. This time I offered my love, a radiant flowing robe that spread out to encompass the planet. Sweeping down, I sought a place to land, a place to lay my heart. Behind me was an echo, an observer, a being of light following me, shadowing me with an invisible link.

I searched eagerly, flying low over the landscape. Nothing appeared. A force seemed to be pushing us, this being of light and I, until in the distance a great mountain appeared. Hope flared inside me. With relief, I sped to the roof of the world. To the Table of Tibet where the Masters lived and trod, a land of Light and Love that shone upon the world.

Introduction

Below me lay a pinnacle. Gladly – hungrily – I swept down and laid my heart upon the highest mountain in the world. And felt it pierce my heart. Startled, I saw the white robes stained crimson, and flew backwards up into the sky, open-mouthed and glaze-eyed.

Far below, a calm blue sea beckoned, calling me. I plummeted down, falling, to enfold myself in the waters of Mother's Love, to lose myself in her caress. And found myself floundering below the surface, unable to breath.

I longed for land, and was spread-eagled on the ground in a red arid land, parched, gazing up at a deep blue sky.

Where else is there to go, I thought, but back to the Air?

Each story is a lesson,

And each lesson a story in …

The physical gaining of knowledge.

PART

ONE

Chapter One

Connection

There was a tingle of anticipation driving out to the land today. As I traveled down the long, winding, dirt road and neared the valley, this tingle of anticipation increased. For an image appeared in my mind of a little point of land at the base of the hill. I had been drawn to it lately, and the thought now arose to meditate there.

Parking the car under the shady trees beside the creek, I wandered along the creek flats, following the car tracks through the long grass, and then wound my way up the hill through the trees to the point of land. Sitting down, I crossed my legs to meditate. Bellbirds chimed overhead and a warm yellow sun shone softly down through the trees. Yet I was restless. I increased my efforts to become calm, but the body wouldn't quieten and neither would the mind. Frustrated, I opened my eyes …

… And sensed a presence. I'd noticed this presence out here before, but never had he felt so close, almost like he was watching me. I twisted round on my seat, peering expectantly through the trees behind, but there was no flash of color or movement to suggest someone was there. Even so, I imagined I could smell the mustiness of his body odor. Idly wondering if he'd walk down and talk to me, I understood he wouldn't, and knew if I went looking for him he wouldn't be found.

Still, the expectation was there, so I stayed, sitting on this flat spot among the trees.

Letting my gaze drift around, I took in the quiet harmony of the bush. The land sloped steeply away from me, down through the trees, and then across a flat, open meadow to the creek. Beside me, gum trees towered through the scattered undergrowth, rising up to spreading branches under a light blue sky. Thin, white, wispy clouds floated above the leaves of their uppermost branches. Feeling settled and calm on my small outpost upon the hillside, I closed my eyes to meditate.

The ground trembled beneath me – and trembled again. I opened my eyes, startled. Was it an earth tremor? I held my breath, waiting. The land was still; the bellbirds piped undisturbed overhead. As I sat there thinking about this strange trembling, I remembered when it had happened once before, and I knew it wasn't just a physical vibration. In another time and place, it had rumbled through the earth, shaking the house as if a huge truck was passing outside.

I closed my eyes, curious and puzzled why it had happened again, when another tremor ran through the ground under me. Keeping my eyes firmly closed, I felt another tremor follow it, and then another, each growing stronger and lasting longer.

These vibrations began to run into my legs and buttocks which were in contact with the earth. They rose up into my body, climbing along my spine and spreading out into my arms and head until my whole body was shaking. It was like sitting on top of a tiny earthquake and I thought I was going to be toppled down the hill! I opened my eyes, ready to brace myself – and saw the land was still. Not a leaf fluttered. The breeze had dropped and bright sunlight was shining down through the trees, falling in dappled patterns upon the grass.

Wondering at what had just happened, I took a deep breath to calm myself, and saw ripples of light spreading out in circles from where I was sitting. With growing fascination, I watched these tumbling waves as they flowed out over the edges of this point of land. Then I realized the waves were echoing the rhythm of the tremors, for the vibrations were continuing, flowing on down the hill and running underneath me, as strong as before.

I decided to join with the vibrations. Willing myself to blend with them, I sent them onwards down the hill. I could follow their course as they continued down towards the creek, but they didn't increase in strength and faded near the front of the land.

I then tried sending them out into the shrubs and trees around me. The waves rippled out, increased in brightness, but disappeared a short way out, leaving me centered in a pool of light.

Unsure of what to do next, I sat there, feeling the vibrations as they ran under me, and into me. The idea came to send them back up the hill to where they were coming from – to where I sensed the presence was. I closed my eyes and, still facing downhill to the creek, focused on the vibrations running beneath me. The odd sensation arose of looking backwards through my heart; I could see the trees on the slope behind me. The scene grew clearer; waves of light were rolling down the hill.

My awareness began to creep up the slope. The waves increased, white clouds of energy billowing past. Cautiously, I inched forward, finding I was gaining momentum. The waves grew stronger. It became harder to keep moving as they started to buffet me, pushing me sideways.

Slowly I waded up through the waves of light, until they were crashing down upon me, and thundering past. I felt like I was swimming against a raging stream and wondered how long I'd be able to keep going. With an effort of will, I concentrated on moving forward.

And then a Light appeared. Looking up the hillside to where it shone brightly above me, I was suddenly surrounded by the Light, and within the Light was the Presence. Connection!

I wanted to stay as long as possible, absorbing this light, this wonderful vibration, but was so full of vigor I couldn't sit still. I jumped up and started to head down to the creek. As I was leaving I felt the Presence again.

It seemed sad and disappointed. I stopped at the bottom of the slope and looked back towards the connection site. Was I leaving too soon? Should I have stayed longer? A longing rose in me. Maybe if I had meditated more, he would've come down.

Perhaps next time …

Chapter Two

Grandfather Goanna Spirit

Having finished work for the afternoon, I was heading back down the hill for a drink and a splash in the creek, when I decided to stop for a moment and catch my breath. I'd been clearing lantana by hand; this large, shallow-rooted shrub had been imported a century ago, and now grew in profusion over the hills, smothering the native flora. Sitting in the heavy shade of a large tree, I took off my hat and work gloves and gazed across the valley to where the distant tree-clad hills were bathed in brilliant sunshine. A soft breeze floated up the hill, drying the sweat on my face.

As I sat there, enjoying the cool breeze and quietness of the valley, I suddenly heard a loud *Scrunch* – like a foot had stepped onto a large pile of dried leaves. I quickly looked around to see what could have made that noise, but the little clearing was still. Just then a presence swept over me, prickling my hair and skin, and a voice gently whispered in my ear, "Grandfather Spirit". And from behind a tree, directly across from where I sat, stepped a large goanna.

He walked boldly into view, heading into the clearing with that ponderous swinging motion of his body, and then turned and scaled the tree he had appeared from behind. I watched as he slowly climbed up the trunk, his claws noisily clutching the bark. Stopping, he turned his head and looked at me. Because of the slope of the land, I was sitting level with him, and staring him straight in the eye.

I had never been so close to a goanna before, less than a dozen steps away, for these large lizards are usually timid creatures, scrambling up trees at the first hint of danger. So it was surprising to see him walk out into the open, and then climb a tree right in front of me! Still, I was careful not to move lest I frighten him. I sat very quietly.

He was the biggest goanna I'd ever seen, nearly man-length from his head on the tree trunk to where his tail curved down to touch the ground, and black-skinned with small patches of color running in designs down his body.

The thought came to sing to him. Worried that it might scare him away, I hesitantly began to softly sound a long *Om* note, but he never moved, gazing at me steadily from his position on the tree. I changed to a mantra, gathering in volume, and then to voicings that just came out spontaneously. The whole time he sat there, eyeing me with a look between friendliness and pity. The last note floated into the silence of the valley. Still, with neither of us moving, we regarded each other.

I found the markings on Grandfather Goanna Spirit fascinating. They reminded me of the dream I'd had that morning – a dream of seeing a boomerang fly in through the door and land on the floor. The dream had come just before waking.

The Dream

We were out the front of the house and my wife was hanging up the washing. Looking up, I saw a huge UFO flying over the house. It was in the shape of a yellow digital clock. I ran through the house and out the back door to get another look, and saw another clock flying in the opposite direction. This time it was a huge red digital clock. (Time flying past and not wanting to miss the early morning on the land?) There were also boomerangs flying in formation through the air, each with a short extra crosspiece attached to a wing.

A boomerang started coming towards me. I expected it to curve away but it kept coming straight on. Hurriedly, I stepped aside and it flew past, straight through the door and into the house. It landed on the floor behind me and I turned to see one wing in deep shadow, and the other lying in the bright, early morning sunlight streaming through the door. The wing in the light was covered in strange, yet attractive, markings.

These markings were similar to the patterns on Grandfather Spirit's tail. Intrigued, I studied the colored designs in detail. From behind his head, a pattern of yellow shapes swept down to meet, and blend into, a series of squares, both yellow and green on the long trunk of his body. These squares broadened out with his girth and then stopped at the base of his tail where a new series of markings began. They were small green shapes that swirled down the length of his tail. I ran my eye back up his body and over the flowing lines of color, highlighted by his black skin.

Finally, I pulled myself out of my reverie. Grandfather Spirit was still looking at me. His eye was now radiating a peace and goodwill like you'd find among good friends – his eye really looked human then.

I enjoyed the moment of closeness and friendliness that came out of the experience with the Being, and then it was time to go. I rolled a mandarin towards him as a gift, expecting it to bounce past him and roll down the hill, but surprisingly it stopped right against the base of the tree. I was even more surprised when he didn't flee with the sudden movement.

Pleased, I rolled two more mandarins towards him. These, too, landed up against the tree. Still he didn't move and I thought, even more so, that this was a special meeting.

I stood up. He shifted on the tree trunk and I quickly stopped, standing still. When he didn't move, I offered a heartfelt blessing and a farewell and, passing the tree he clung to, walked off down the hill.

Chapter Three

The Snake

Twilight was deepening as I made my way slowly back to the car along the narrow bush track. Trees hung over the pathway, making it gloomier and darker still. Dirty and sweat soaked, I had worked in the hot summer's afternoon clearing lantana until it was almost too dark to see.

A long, thin, black shadow lay across the pathway.

I slowed, peering towards it. It was too dark to tell exactly what it was, but I wasn't too concerned. Many times I had cautiously approached a snake-like object on the ground, only to find it was an old branch or twig lying there. Besides, I thought, if it was a snake it would slither off before I got too close. It was high summer and they move quickly in the heat. I stamped along, thumping my feet onto the ground and letting it know, if it was a snake, that I was coming. It didn't move. Still, as I neared it, I became wary. I didn't want to step over it just in case it was a snake.

Bent over, I was slowly moving towards it, squinting through the gloom, until my nose was almost within arm's reach of it, when suddenly I realized – it was a snake! Startled, I straightened up, and in one quick movement leapt back! And put a surprising amount of distance between myself and the snake in that one big jump! Without taking my eyes from it, I slowly took a few backward steps, putting a little more space between the two of us.

I stood silently, staring down at the black shadow of the snake lying stretched across the bush track. There was a strange tingling sensation around my feet and I decided to move even further back, but then thought, "No, I'll stay here." Courage arose, and I knew I was safe – safe, at least, from my own mental processes. And oddly enough, I was calm – the heart rate and breath hadn't accelerated at all.

But what was I to do? It was nearly dark and here was this snake blocking my path! I looked back along the track the way I had come, and then up through the trees to where the first stars were shining. There were only about ten minutes of light left, and almost none within the heavy shade of the thick trees surrounding me. To avoid the snake, I'd have to backtrack and then swing up and around the hillside, battling my way through the trees and lantana and getting torn and scratched in the process, for there was no other easy way back to the car from where I stood. Not the end to the evening I had hoped for.

Yet it seemed so unusual for a snake to be lying there, not moving on the pathway, and I wondered why. The idea arose to contact it. I mentally projected a friendly, "Hello," towards it. There was no answer. The snake lay still. I gathered myself and sent as strong a greeting as I could. Did I pick up a slight response?

Then an image appeared in my mind of the grassy connection site nearby, sitting amongst the trees higher up on the hillside, and the thought came, "Send it as a rumble through the ground."

Gathering my greeting, I sent it down to my feet and into the earth, willing it towards the snake. He began to move – oh, so slowly – inching himself off the path. It had worked! I watched, peering through the deepening gloom, unsure at first if he really was moving. But he was!

As he began to slowly slither off the track, I felt a tearing sensation in my chest. It started in the left side, ripping across to my right, like someone was slowly opening a huge line in my chest.

When the snake's tail appeared on the track, his body easing over the side, the tearing sensation began to subside and it felt like a weight was being lifted off my chest. I took a few breaths, surprised at how deeply and freely I was breathing, and realized that this opening up had been timed to the rhythm of the snake as it'd crawled off the path.

The end of its tail began to slide off the track. I quickly walked up to where the snake had lain, feeling his impression under my feet and staring after him until his thin, black length had vanished into the gloom under the trees.

Chapter Four

Tree Spirit

Early one summer's morning, I decided to climb the hill at the back of the land. It's a long walk and I was well prepared with a bucket containing a water bottle, snacks, a mobile phone and other bits and pieces. A solid gum tree branch that'd come to hand made an excellent walking staff. Leaving the car near the creek, I walked along the creek flats and up the hill, slowly making my way through the tangled undergrowth and thick trees, following an old, overgrown logging track up to where a ridge meets the hill. This ridge starts near the gate, rising up and leveling out to join with the hill at the back of the land, about one third of the way up its slope.

Climbing out onto the ridge, I rested in the shade of a tree, sipping from the water bottle and looking across the valley. The air was fresh and clean up here, especially after tramping over the musty, dead leaves of the forest and through the dense undergrowth.

The next section of the hill was very steep. The old logging track had been recently widened by a bull-dozer, making it clear walking. Gathering my gear, I set off again. Trees had also been felled, and I passed new stumps with clumps of branches lying in untidy heaps beside the track. Pieces of white quartz had been unearthed by the bulldozer and lay scattered across the broken ground.

Part One

Pushing into the forest past the end of the dozer tracks, I tried to remember the landmarks of previous visits. A tall hollowed tree stump soon appeared, an obvious and familiar marker, and I knew I was on the right track. More than once I stopped to rest, facing downhill to ease my aching calf muscles, and each time the view had expanded across the valley.

The top of the hill appeared through the trees and I looked for somewhere to pause before the final climb. A little pathway drew me in. Wandering through the trees along this winding animal trail, I came to where a huge gum tree towered overhead. Impressed, I gazed up at its wide white trunk that soared into the canopy, following the tree's line until it disappeared amongst the leaves and branches of the surrounding trees. With the sweat running down my face, I sat down on a litter of soft leaves and took off my hat. The day was warming up. There was a very pleasant feel to this spot and I was happy to sit among the rainforest trees, listening to the birdcalls chirping through the stillness, and surrounded by the peace of the bush.

Some old branches were lying on the ground in front of me. They seemed unusually arranged to my eye, as if they'd been deliberately placed around this level sitting area, rather than having been washed down. With a start, I remembered that I was the one who had put them there! For I was sitting in exactly the same spot as the last time I had climbed up here. It must have been over a year ago. Worried that this sloping area beside the tree might erode with the rains, I had placed branches around it to hold the soil in. But I was struck by how odd it was to stumble across it again! There was nothing remarkable about the pathway, no obvious landmark to indicate its existence, yet I had been strongly drawn to it once more. Bidding farewell to the tree, I headed back along the animal trail and up towards the top.

An open, grassy, crescent-shaped area with a wonderful view over the valley lay just before the crest of the hill. Every time I walk past it, enjoying its delicate feel, a friend would come to mind. I could imagine him living up here in a little dwelling, high above the valley, with a big view over the distant hills.

Another short steep walk brought me to a rusty barbed wire fence that runs along the top of the hill. Carefully climbing through, I followed it up to where a pile of jumbled rocks marks the peak. Balancing atop the rocks, I peered down through the trees, searching for a tall flat rock lying just off the side of the hill. The first time I had sat there all thoughts had stopped, the mind going instantly calm. But I couldn't see the rock; everything seemed different ... Then I spotted it amidst the trees and scrambled down to it. The fine dark soil was dry and powdery, a layer of dead leaves slippery underfoot.

The Sitting Rock

I was pleased and slightly apprehensive when I walked up to the sitting rock. After the connection site, I was wondering what would happen next. Hoisting myself up onto the large, red, squarish rock, I brushed aside some loose leaves and sat down, letting my eyes drift through the forest. I was expecting to find a particular vibration here, but it was quiet – very quiet. There was a vibration … but different, somehow.

Peeping through the trees was the blue tarp on the cottage of a neighboring property. This cottage stands beside a healing site – the female companion to my hilltop lookout. As the sound of a car drove up the steep driveway to the small house, I fell into meditation. It ended a short while later when the car drove away.

Sitting on the rock after meditating, I felt faintly disappointed. There'd been the feeling that something profound would happen this morning – a sense of expectancy. Was there someone here I was to meet? Would he leave me a sign? I didn't want to second guess events, or wish too hard, but his presence was absent.

Feeling jittery, and not wanting to walk back yet, I gazed through the trees and across the valley, enjoying the solitude of the hilltop, when my eyes fell upon a little path that wound its way down through the lantana – an animal tunnel through the undergrowth that called. I considered it. There was no way down to the creek through the mass of lantana that covered that side of the hill. I had tried several times to climb up that way – without success. Still, I thought, it couldn't hurt to explore a little.

Following the tunnel down through the undergrowth, and ducking low to avoid getting snagged on the prickly lantana, I came out to stand before another animal tunnel that led further down the hill. At the far end of that short tunnel, I could see another pathway opening up beyond it, going deeper into the lantana.

I stood debating whether to go further down or climb back up. Walking down was easy, but it would be difficult climbing up the steep hill, and each section took me further away from the top. I looked up the hill behind me, judging the distance to its peak. Deciding to go back, I turned around but my feet wouldn't move. I stood straining to walk forward until, with great difficulty, I took a few short steps.

Intrigued, I faced downhill. There was no impediment as I walked towards the mouth of the tunnel. I turned and went to walk up the hill. Again my feet felt like lead and it took all my strength to move forward. Giving in to the obvious, I allowed my feet to carry me down through the tunnel in the lantana, following the pathways as they opened up before me.

The Pine Trees

I stopped for a rest on a flat spot under a tree. This area was fairly clear of lantana and I could follow the curve of the land as it swung around the hill below me.

Something sharp pierced my pants. I shifted over and found I was sitting on long, brown leaves with sharp, serrated edges. They were scattered all around the base of the tree. Looking up, I saw I was sitting under a tall pine tree. Surprised, I realized that this pine tree is clearly visible from the creek at the front of the land, perched high on the side of the hill, a feature amongst the other trees. And nearby was another pine! At least I knew where I was.

It was a gorgeous spot. The light, softened by the shady trees, threw a gentle greenish tinge down upon the landscape. The trees and ferns and plants all looked so alive; even the rocks seemed to glow in the tropical twilight. The blue of sky peeped through the canopy of trees, adding an almost magical quality to it. Peace crept into my soul and I fell into the moment. What a wonderful place to share with others, I thought, and what a difficult trek it was to get here!

It was time to get going again. Beside me ran a narrow rock-strewn gully with stag horns and ferns clinging to its sides. Although it was very steep, it was also fairly free of undergrowth. Deciding to follow it down, rather than climbing through the animal tunnels in the lantana, I gingerly clambered over the loose rocks, slowly making my way under the shelter of the tropical trees until the gully, too, became impassable. I stopped, looking for a way to continue. Daylight peeped through a gap in the lantana. Perhaps there was a way down after all! Scrambling through on my hands and knees, I crawled beneath the lantana and came out on a flat, open corner of the hillside.

There was a wide view out over the valley from here. I had never seen it from this perspective before, and I stood enjoying the scenery and cool breeze after the close confines of the lantana. From my vantage point, I ran my eye down the hillside and over the treetops.

Somewhere through the lantana, not far below me, was the connection site. At the bottom of the hill were the creek flats stretching away towards the road, and to my right was the cottage with the blue tarp. I was surprised how far down the hill I'd come.

I started searching for an opening in the huge green tangle before me. Unable to see one, I circled round this small spur on the side of the hill, seeking a tunnel, a path, a break in the undergrowth, anything that would lead me down the last section of the hill and back to the creek, for I didn't want to face the difficulty of climbing back to the top through the matted lantana. After circling the spur of land for the third frustrating time, I realized I had no choice. I had to climb back up.

Already tired after the long walk, the thought of climbing back up was daunting, but there was nothing for it, so I simply started. Unable to find my way back to the gully, or the tunnels I'd come down, I crashed my way through the undergrowth. My feet couldn't grip on the dry leaf-covered ground and I kept slipping backwards; the long clinging tendrils of lantana clutched at me as I struggled upwards. Hanging onto tree branches and bushes, I pulled myself forward.

Eventually the lantana became so thick that I had to crawl underneath it. I would find an opening and crawl a short distance, to lie panting on the ground, my face pressed against the dry leaves – and then forward again. Dragging the bucket through the lantana became a hassle, and the staff caught their trailing branches as I struggled on.

The Pine Trees Again

I lay gasping for breath on a flat spot, waiting for my heartbeat to slow down. It was time for a longer rest. Drenched in sweat, I stretched out and felt something sharp digging into my back. Wriggling over, I saw long, brown leaves lying on the ground around me. Remembering the unusual shape, I looked up and saw I was lying under the same pine tree as before! I had to laugh aloud at the coincidence and felt quite friendly towards the tree. Sitting up, I ran my eyes over this tiny hidden glade, tucked up against the side of the hill. There was a fairy-like quality to the softly shadowed landscape and I gazed around, drinking in the colors. It was peaceful and still.

I continued on. Not long afterwards I discarded the bucket. I'd crushed it against my knee while scrambling up, and finally I discarded the staff as well, for it kept catching on the lantana and holding me back. Gripping only the mobile phone, for I feared losing it would have me scratching around the hillside trying to find it, I continued painfully up the slope.

Time became irrelevant. The journey became a series of short bursts of crawling through the undergrowth, and then stopping to regain my breath. At one point I'd had enough. I stretched out exhausted on the ground. But what could I do? I couldn't go back down and I couldn't stay there on the hillside. Cursing and swearing, I pushed myself on.

It seemed forever before I came out into the relatively cleared area below the summit. There was the sitting rock, just a few more short climbs ahead. It took a while to reclaim that distance on my hands and knees until, finally, I was able to stand and stagger the rest of the way to the peak.

By the time I'd walked back down the hill to the car, the sun was high overhead. I stood on the creek flats, looking over the connection site hidden amongst the trees, and past the open spur of land, to the pine tree that stood out clearly against the sky. Remembering the tropical twilight there, I thought how much of the morning had been spent on that steep hillside, clambering around through the dense undergrowth.

Tree Spirit

Later in the week, my wife and I were sitting outside in the cool of the summer evening. I was talking about the trip up and down the hillside when she said she could smell something fragrant. I looked over and saw a tall dark shadow behind her.

When I peered into this shadow, an image arose of the pine trees standing on the hillside, and I remembered the soft light that had filtered down onto the rocks and ferns clinging to the narrow gully. I could almost smell the humus of the forest floor. Was this a spirit from there? Had he followed me home? He issued a strong male presence, but I didn't sense anything sinister about him.

It turned out that both my wife and one of the children had noticed shadows in the house over the last week or so. A friend had also said that there had been a shadow in her house lately, also.

For the next few days, the presence followed me everywhere around the house. If I turned quickly I'd almost walk into him, and would have to step awkwardly around him. I didn't mind; he seemed curious more than anything.

One morning he followed me into the bathroom when I went to clean my teeth. He was right on top of me, leaning over my shoulder inquisitively as I bent over the washbasin. Feeling crowded, I asked him to give me more room. He retreated, and I saw little of him after that …

I did notice him occasionally near the trees where we'd sit in the afternoons, although sometimes I would notice a faint shadow inside, too. During this time, an artist friend pointed out a face on a tree in our yard. It resembled a wolf's face. (I can feel the gentle presence of the Tree Spirit watching over my shoulder now as I write this.)

He Goes Home

The next weekend, I climbed back up the ridge to take photographs of the trees that had been cut down and where the bulldozer had been. I was about to walk back when I thought that if I went a little higher up, I'd get a better picture of the tree stumps. Turning up the hill,

I saw a huge shimmering oval of energy beside a large apple gum tree on the edge of the dozer tracks. The energy made the colors of the bush behind twist and swirl, like pebbles dropped in a still pool. From out of the midst of that swirling energy did the Tree Spirit bid me farewell. I hadn't known he'd followed me out here! Three times he hailed me: I am here; Farewell; and Good Cheer; and with that he flew back to the other side of the hill where the pine trees stood.

Chapter Five

The Inner Earth Warrior

While sitting in meditation one morning, connecting with the earth, I was suddenly drawn down into the ground. In a cavern, far below the surface, sat a warrior, cleaning his weapons. He looked up. His presence was one of direct challenge to me. Provocative. Inflaming. Would I fight? Would I flee? I stood still and didn't react either way, having learnt that such reactions invariably are the incorrect response.

With the warrior trying to unnerve me with his presence, I projected peace toward him in a friendly gesture. This was ignored. I then gently reached out to touch his aura, trying to dissolve his anger, his hurt. But this meant little to him. Here was a soldier: trained, professional. His mind, stance and presence were of a dedicated, and lifelong, attunement to War. He seemed intent upon trying to rile me by exerting a steady, needling pressure. Yet, I had no intention of fighting or getting angry.

So, I waited. Did he have a message for me, I wondered? Would we talk? But he simply sat there, looking down as he cleaned his weapons, and challenging me with his presence.

I peered around in curiosity at the cavern. Smooth, cream-coloured walls swept back over to a domed ceiling and stacked on the floor were huge piles of weapons and jewels. They glowed in a range of glittering colors that bedazzled the eye.

I turned back to the Inner Earth Warrior sitting quietly nearby. Although he was calmly polishing his weapons as soldiers have always done, he also seemed to be eternally vigilant. I felt that he could change into a killing machine instantly, having no regard for any previous contact that you may have had with him. If the order came to attack, he would – no second thoughts, no hesitations, instantly into warrior mode – adrenalin pumping, mind focused. Battle Joy! He let me know it too … and then waited for my response.

Yet, I remained calm, realizing he couldn't hurt me, but only scare me.

After Thoughts

After this experience, I had a great deal of trouble grounding myself, in getting that connection with the earth again. It became disconcerting. I could also sense the Warrior still around me, and each time I would feel his presence or see his face in my mind, the feelings of Attack (Battle Joy) would arise.

Until I understood that they were *my* feelings – and not his!

(Was this presence known to me in another time?)

The realization came that the only way to maintain Peace in myself, was to remove the 'attack mode' from my own consciousness. It was at this point that I started regarding him as my friend.

Yet, even when I realized this, there was no let up from him, no recognition of the rapport between us, no lessening of the pressure. And this is still the feeling I get at writing – welcoming but hostile, calm yet instantly changeable … and eternally vigilant.

But I cannot help but think of him as a friend, for I am grateful for what he showed me.

Chapter Six

The Old Warrior

NTA: Help

NTA: Have a dilemma: I keep getting sucked into trying to heal these old warriors, the ancient ones – who's ego is eating away their bodies. They ask for healing, but never intend to use it …..just keep their old ways – zapping and battling among themselves. Am losing another one, a powerhouse.

DreamSnake: A story to help pick up your spirits NTA? I'll e-mail it to you now~

NTA: He is one of the most powerful healers on the planet, watched him move mountains, but his personal health is just a string of energy he sucks from those he heals. Dilemma

DreamSnake: is he dying?

NTA: Yes, he is walking death, for several years now

DreamSnake: sent it NTA

NTA: He has more scars than bòdy left - but won't give up the ego, loves to zap anyone who wants to play.

DreamSnake: He can't release...you can't help him release...Then you've got to fight him...make/show him to put his defences down~he has nothing to fear!

NTA: DreamSnake: I loved the story - was great

DreamSnake: ~Smiles~

NTA: I did that, everything I could think of – he has been in and out of my body several times, searched every inch to find anything he could use. Finally booted him out, was tickling my heart a little too much. He found no fear, but he still continues.

NTA: I just don't know what to do – perhaps just wait and send flowers, any ideas

DreamSnake: Too powerful to beat...too egotistical to let go..True..a dilemma... need to think on it~

DreamSnake: While we're thinking I'll post up that story...might help..*S*

DreamSnake: A young fellow was working out west. Once you get off the coast there ain't much around anywhere... grass lands and desert ....Well, the abos took a liking to him and let him sit in on their corroborees. One time they said he could watch but not join in. From outside the circle he could see one elder jumping and dancing on the other side of the fire.

Then the fellow disappeared...He appeared on the other side of the fire...and then disappeared... and re-appeared again on the other side....He'd taped it and sent it to his mother. Won't let anyone hear it, though.

DreamSnake: NTA...what is they're purpose here?

NTA: thinking hard on "their purpose here". Balance come to mind – part of trios – 1st part light workers, second part energy workers and third part – power of the ancient warrior (magic of visions).

DreamSnake: What do you do NTA..if I may ask?..*S*

NTA: I am a neutral (energy worker). Task is to unite light beings and warriors to perform given tasks for alignment.

NTA: An ancient warrior, like this being has the power and wisdom to lift Uluru and activate the earth crystals, if the task were asked. Do you understand my dilemma - we need him.

DreamSnake: but???

DreamSnake: but his ego...???

DreamSnake: NTA....it's early afternoon here...early tomorrow morning I can go and ask.

DreamSnake: I just need more information.

NTA: E mail when you get an answer – a real dilemma for me – not getting any help on this one - thank you

DreamSnake: NTA...how are you losing this old warrior?

DreamSnake: NTA.. I'd love to ask you more questions but I fear this place may be too public..*S*

NTA: DreamSnake …thanks – I never have fear of public, as you have probably noticed….lol

DreamSnake: OK...methinks there is a need to ask some distant powers for the answer.

NTA: I have met many of his kind, but never any of the strength of his energy. Was beginning to think it was Merlin incarnate, but ego is the difference.

NTA: The blacks may know of him – am sure they do

DreamSnake: Yes, was thinking the same thing of the blacks...*S*...You could ask Galactic Federation for an answer~I'm having the feeling that the answer is there~

DreamSnake: the ego part is baffling....strange to imagine someone so powerful wrapped in ego...seems it'd be to his detriment...he is needed but he needs to release his ego...would he die if he released [his ego] or is he afraid that that's what would happen?

NTA: that is the dilemma, yes to your last line, both is the answer. We need him to stick around for 15 more years. He just laughs at it, like an old warrior who seeks the fight.

DreamSnake: Sounds like he needs a new body~

NTA: He was here, on a small energy job, his body took both my and a powerful light worker's energy just to walk a quarter mile to where we needed to go. He is not walking without strong energy around to assist. (Was thinking Galactic might requisition him something, but afraid they will send him elsewhere.)

DreamSnake: Stand him on the energy lines and I'll ask the blacks to sing him.

NTA: Gonna have to do that without his knowledge, and I hate doing that. I know he would fight them. Dilemma plus

DreamSnake: So he's caught no matter how you look at it. He's trapped within himself~

DreamSnake: Well, I'll go and ask and see what happens...thanks for the info... Spirit Will Provide

NTA: if the blacks agree, ask them for a description of an object, I will tell him of it, so he can go to it. Warn them that he is powerful.

DreamSnake: Will do...if not I'll ask B. of the Galactic Federation.. perhaps he has guidance.

DreamSnake: A black circular rock......molded (?) in the ground...ask him to walk around it three times and face the east... Bow down and give thanks for guidance. Then ask him to release to the universe the power that he has been given. And pray for guidance for the next step...

NTA: TO THE PUBLIC: If you read this, my intent is for sharing, lessons for learning – spirit is spirit – we all share the journey. Good journey all.

Chapter Seven

The Dreamsnake

After early summer rains, the weather turned scorching hot. Sunday morning dawned comfortably cool, with scattered clouds taking the sting out of the sun. Today, a group of us were going to explore a site once used by the indigenous tribes to birth their babies.

We met at a park beside a historical museum with people from outside the district joining us as well, until thirty-four people had gathered. Piling into our cars, we followed the leader out of town and into a farming area, where the paved road petered out into a dirt road that ran beside a twisting stream. The farmland gave way to forest, the bumpy road winding its way through pine-covered hills.

Parking on a side road near the creek, we gathered for a talk where Brett, our guide for the day, explained the protocols required for entering and visiting such a site. Under the native law that had once existed here, men and women kept separate sites and ceremonies, but today, we were assured, both groups were welcome. As Brett spoke, he held a tall wooden staff in his hand with a white feather sitting on the top.

I later learned that the feather – a cockatoo's feather – was a sign of the last elder of the tribe and Brett, as custodian, had continued the custom. Looking at the feather, he said that as this one was getting ragged, he'd have to replace it soon. A lady, standing near him, offered a white cockatoo feather from her own staff, and this was secured atop his own.

With Brett leading the way, the group was soon meandering down into the narrow valley. We followed the pathway beside the stream as it wound its way along the flat creek floor, over the rocks and around the pools joined together by the thin ribbon of trickling water. It's a pretty spot, a little tropical haven filled with moss-covered rocks, and shaded by the trees and palms that adorn the valley's sides.

After walking some distance down the creek, Brett stopped beside a tall outcrop of rock that leaned out over the water, and waited for the group to catch up. When we had gathered, he told us that when the sunlight is falling in the right direction, it reflects off the water and throws a rainbow up against the overhanging rock.

He then performed a ceremony beside the Rainbow Rock, asking permission to enter. Drawing a circle on the sand in the middle of the creek with his staff, he stood it upright in the center. Taking small stones from a leather pouch around his neck, he shook them together in his cupped hands as he slowly walked around the staff. (Later, he explained to me that these are the sacred stones of Dai'ar-ba'ri-wun'daman – Dreamtime stones that tell you everything you want to know when asking for guidance.)

Opening his hands, he dropped the stones within the circle while we quietly waited, respectful and expectant. Bending down, he carefully examined them as they lay on the sand. As he began to gather them, I heard my name being called. Curiously, I glanced around, wondering who it was, when I heard my name being called again.

Listening intently to see if I could pinpoint where the soft voice was coming from, I noticed that Brett had hesitated, carefully weighing a stone in his hand with a concentrated expression upon his face. He seemed to be considering, looking upwards. Then he picked up the next stone, and the next, paused a few moments and then quickly picked up the rest. Straightening up, he told us that the signs were that we were welcome to enter, and that there was nothing that hindered our way in.

He went on to say that there was someone here who was extremely psychic. He didn't know who it was but that person may want to sit on the rock above the pool and meditate. I looked around at the faces, knowing there were a lot of intuitive people here and wondering whom it might be, for I had already made up my mind to find a quiet place to sit. He also said that there were two non-believers here and asked that they listen, and respect, what they see and hear today. (Two people did indeed leave not long after, with one overheard to be making disparaging comments.)

He then led us in a chant in the old language, a gentle passage affirming life that subtly changed the atmosphere within the group. Although the melody of the chant has been lost, the words remain, having been recorded and passed down.

A short distance away was a massive slab of rock that spanned the creek, the waters having eroded a path down through it. This, Brett assured us, was the place. We filed through the narrow opening in the tall rock, walking beside a long, shallow pool. The opening widened out, and I saw the creek falling into a small round pool cut deep into this block of rock. Beyond it, and lower down, was another larger pool. Almost immediately people scattered, making room for the others who followed. I moved to my right and scaled a steep rock face to the highest part over the round pool, a rocky peak about two man-heights above the water.

Sitting down cross-legged, I had a perfect view of the pool below. It was circular, created by the action of the waters flowing across this huge rock that bridges the banks. Large enough for several people to splash in, the water was crystal clear, with red rocks lining the bottom. The creek was filled with these red rocks, large boulders and small stones, a deep rich colour, almost black in places. On the other side of the pool, two ladies were sitting where the waters had smoothed the rock into a low, flowing waveform.

From the circular pool, the water flowed down a sloping rock face and into a large sandy pool around which many of the people were sitting. This large pool spreads out towards two cliff faces, topped with trees and palms. The creek dropped down between these cliffs and out of sight.

I felt a bit self-conscious, sitting there perched above the pool after what Brett had said earlier, yet felt calm.

The rocks dug into my ankles, and I wriggled around trying to get comfortable. My sunglasses irritated me and I took them off, to put them back on again. Someone sat beside me and I closed my eyes in meditation, trying to ignore the uncomfortable rocks beneath. It was very quiet, as if the people were reluctant to disturb the silence of the pools.

Faint energies were rolling down the creek, like a soft breeze sighing over the water. I opened my eyes and looked down between the cliffs, seeing the gentle green of palm trees and ferns, the blue of sky, and wondering where the energy was coming from. I closed my eyes again.

A vague uneasiness began to rise. A sob unexpectedly caught in my throat and my eyes began to fill with tears. A low soft chant drifted by. I heard a woman's voice singing. It lingered sadly in my heart and then faded, to reappear, this time with more voices joining in.

As I sat on the rock, listening to the singing echoing in and out of my consciousness, I become aware of the water tumbling into the pool below. The sound of the water grew louder and louder until it'd drowned out the other senses, and there was only the presence of the rushing water. Gently it tugged at me. Turning toward it, I hesitantly began following its guidance. My consciousness was drawn to the opposite bank where a cliff face dropped down into the lower pool. As I beheld the large rocky face, the energy deepened and a door – or gap – appeared in the rock. I stared at it, waiting, hoping it would open. It didn't, and I was aware again of sitting above the pool with the sharp rocks digging into my ankles.

The sound of the women's chanting floated by again. I tried to memorize the melody and the words, singing it softly it to myself as it drifted in and out. There was a gentle wailing tone to the voices, as if the song had been continuing for hours and they were tired. (In a later conversation, several people mentioned visiting the mining tunnels beneath the town and hearing unusual noises, or voices. They, too, had been wearing glasses; the suggestion being that the metal in the frames amplified the sound.)

Opening my eyes, I gazed around at the landscape and the people contentedly lazing about the pools. It was a peaceful scene. As my eyes came to rest on the water in the circular pool below, I had the desire to get wet – and quickly. Cautiously clambering down the steep rock face to the bottom, I passed Brett who made a diving motion with his hand. I nodded, smiling. The two ladies were still sitting on the edge of the pool, dangling their feet in the water. Stripping off my shirt and leaving my jeans on, I hesitated, looking into the clear waters, unsure whether to jump in or just slide in slowly, when I saw another lady sitting where the creek flows into the pool, the water swirling around her. Taking a deep breath, I dived in.

The water was beautiful, cool and smooth, hugging me like a silken skin. The dive took me toward the gravely bottom, and I used my hands to pull myself up short from touching it. Feeling the magnificence of the water around me, I lingered under the surface, enjoying its first touch. I peered around but everything was blurry. It was hard to distinguish anything clearly on the bottom or the steep sides of the pool, so I turned towards the surface, and became transfixed. Sunlight streamed down into the water, shattering into thin beams as it struck the surface, the colours of the rainbow appearing amongst the spreading rays of light.

Slowly, I started to lift towards the surface. I kicked my feet and released the air in my lungs to stay under longer, and make this magical moment last as long as possible, until I had to take a breath. Popping up, I stood on the pebbled bottom with the water up to my chest, the two ladies sitting on the edge of the pool watching. Taking another breath, I released myself back into the embrace of the water. It was tranquil in the silence under the surface, and the essence of mother's love came strongly through.

I splashed lazily around in the pool for a while, enjoying the feel of the soft water molding itself to my body. Looking over, I saw the lady who was sitting on the ledge where the water entered the pool start to cry. Her eyes were tightly closed, screwed up, and I wondered if that was the ledge where the ladies used to sit to birth their babies.

Words began to rise in my throat, but I forced them down. Again they arose, and I examined them. They wanted to be said, yet I was aware of the two ladies beside me, sitting with their feet in the pool. And then the words came, "Let go of the pain."

PART ONE

The lady on the ledge kept on crying and I spoke the words again, more loudly over the sound of the running water. She opened her eyes and angrily replied and I, finding no more words to say, moved back to the center of the pool. Strangely, I didn't feel unsettled by the exchange. There was a sense of detachment, and it was comforting standing there in the cool waters.

(This lady explained to me afterwards that she had re-experienced dying in childbirth while sitting there on the ledge. This, she said, related to the birth of her first child in this life. She looked drawn around the eyes when telling me this, yet her mouth was contented and relieved, and although she moved away tiredly, her movements were graceful.)

A small white stone on the bottom caught my eye. I dived down, grabbed at it and missed, stirring up leaves and dirt on the bottom. I waited for the water to clear and tried again … and missed again. I felt a bit embarrassed in front of the two ladies, but there was nothing for it but to dive down once more. And then up it came, a little milky-white piece of quartz as large as my thumb. I was strongly attracted to it, and could feel it drawing me as I gazed down at it. Lifting my hand, I placed the stone against my forehead, and a sense of power flowed into me.

As I stood in the water with the crystal against my forehead, I saw a rock wall before me. It was the wall I had been sitting atop earlier when the women's chanting had come floating through. The wall was now pulling me towards it. I slowly waded through the water, the pebbles sliding under my feet, and stood before it. Earlier, while swimming in the pool, someone had seen a spider on the rock wall and had asked Brett if it was significant. He had replied that it was. I eyed the wall warily but didn't see one, and with the thumb-sized crystal firmly held in my hand, slowly leaned forward to place my forehead against the wall's hard surface. A pathway of light opened up. My mind began to run down along this pathway and then abruptly it stopped.

I stood back surprised, the light echoing in my mind. Leaning forward, I again lightly touched the wall with my forehead, and again the pathway opened up – and then stopped. For the third time, I tried to follow the light back to its source, but it took me no nearer than the other times.

Standing before the wall, and weighing the crystal in my hand, I was contemplating what had just happened when I heard a voice in my ear say, "Second chakra." I listened, and heard it again. Puzzled, I wondered what it could mean.

One of the ladies sitting on the edge of the pool told me during lunch that the second chakra is where the baby, or birthing energy, comes from. She explained how the energy sweeps down through the body and out the birthing canal. She also mentioned the need to draw this energy back up afterwards.

The group began to file slowly back up the creek. I lingered behind with a few others, letting the crowd move ahead. We passed the Rainbow Rock, and the friend I was chatting to moved to stand in front of it. I walked further on to give her personal space, and waited. The remaining couples wandered past, their voices diminishing, leaving only the stillness of the bush and the sound of the flowing stream.

I watched as she stood on the sand across from the Rainbow Rock, palms pointing down and out, to splash through the shallow water and stop before it. Raising her hands, she laid them on the rock face and then leaned forward to press her forehead against it. For a moment she held the pose, and then stepped back with a mingled look of surprise and contemplation on her face.

I waited for her to return and then we started walking up the creek together. I was curious to see if she would mention what had happened, when I felt a strong pull from behind. I looked back along the creek towards the pools and felt the tug again.

Too strong to be ignored, I made the excuse that I'd forgotten something, and walked quickly back to the sandy strip in the middle of the creek opposite the Rainbow Rock. I paused, sensing the energies, wondering why I was here. The feeling was one of *something left behind*, or *something left undone*. There was no-one here now … perhaps someone had left something at the pools?

As I stood there, waiting and wondering, the sun peeped out overhead between the trees, shining down into this little valley. When I'd been with the group near the Rainbow Rock earlier, clouds had been across the sky. Now the sun was shining down on to the waters of the creek and throwing its rays up onto the overhanging rock before me. Waving lines of yellow light flickered upon its face. The lines didn't separate into rainbow colours but I was pleased to have seen the reflections. I looked up. The sun had passed its noon position. This was the time, I saw, when the sunlight would throw up reflections off the water.

Leaning on my staff, I realised that this must be very near the spot where Brett had cast the stones, and I scanned the sand around me. Turning to leave, I bumped the end of my staff on a rock, the sharp sound startling me with its loudness. A vibration ran through the creek bed. Feeling the vibration running under my feet, and baffled why the sound had caused such an effect, I glanced up to see a huge snake racing up the creek from the direction of the birthing pools. It was enormous, a visionary snake of rainbow colours, undulating up and down and moving with incredible swiftness. Then it stopped and rose up, towering over me – its huge mouth wide open.

I gazed up, frozen, looking into the blackness of it gaping mouth. Two enormous, white fangs protruded from its top jaw. I waited for what would happen next, wondering if it would swallow me, knowing it couldn't hurt me. The snake didn't move. Gently, I extended a greeting to it. There was no response. I waited. It stood unmoving.

Perhaps I should be afraid, I thought, staring up in to the vast cavern of its mouth, and wondered what it would be like to be drawn inside the blackness of its body. But, mentally, the ground I was standing on was firm. Out of the corner of my eye, I saw splashes of colour on the snake's body as it ran down to its tail, and glimpses of the creek beyond. Running out of ideas on how to get it to respond, I stood silently looking up at it, and it down at me ...

Feeling it was time to go, I acknowledged the Snake, thanked Spirit for the vision and turned up the creek to find my friend still waiting for me. She asked, with a grin, if I'd found what I'd left behind. I thought for a moment and, thinking that Snake wasn't a good answer, said, "Self ... just facing self." She looked at me a bit oddly.

For I had dreamt of this Snake a few weeks before, and the advice given about the dream was that *snake* often represented *self*. It had appeared in the dream in exactly the same way too – standing over me, huge, its mouth gaping open, and I assumed that the emotions brought forward at the meeting today – of joy at the vision, and fear of what might happen – were simply reflecting the inner me.

But now, I wonder if it is somehow linked to the energy of the Dreamtime.

Chapter Eight

Spirals

31 December 2000

Dragon 7.00 pm

We were waiting in the twilight on New Year's Eve for the fire ceremony to begin, the finale of the week-long folk festival. Sitting on the hillside under lowering clouds, and surrounded by thousands of people, my wife and I looked down to the center of this natural amphitheater where a tall wooden tower stood – the climax for the night. Across from us was a large lighted stage where the musicians were warming up and tuning their instruments.

Grey clouds were rolling in, threatening to start drizzling. Last year, it'd rained until just before the fire ceremony had started, and began raining again just after it'd finished. I could sense a buzz of expectation among the crowd that this year would be the same. Behind us people continued to file in, moving higher up on the hillside. Tired of waiting for the performance to start, I closed my eyes in meditation.

A dragon appeared – long, thin and black – flying against a blue sky. I was rather startled, to say the least, and expected it to disappear! But surprise didn't make the vision fail, so I watched it, trying to memorize as much of it as I could while it was there.

Shaded in dark colours, it had a large horse-shaped head and triangular protuberances along its back. Its nostrils were flared, but I don't remember if I saw smoke. Twirling upright upon its coiled tail, it spun in the air, quickly moving to a different position in the sky, zipping back and forth across my field of vision. I kept expecting it to fly away, but it seemed to be teasing me, ducking hither and yon.

What surprised me was how thin the dragon was. I was expecting it to be the classic, fat-bellied shape with wings – but, unlike the fantasy books, I didn't see any wings. Just this long, thin, black snake.

I opened my eyes, looking down over the heads of the people to the arena below, and up to the stage filled with colorfully-dressed performers. Closing my eyes, I saw the dragon again, spinning in spirals across my inner vision and whirling around itself in a cloudless sky. Strangely, I had traced the energy spiral in a tipi earlier.

Tipi 5.00 pm

The outer covering of the tipi had been removed, leaving only the poles and a string of black, red and yellow flags wrapped around the top. It stood beside two covered tipis that were still being used. I was looking for a place to rest and found a shaded slope beside the tipis, tucked down in a quiet hollow away from the festival tents. I lay back on the grass, feeling the earth beneath, but there was a pull, so I sat up in meditation.

When I opened my eyes I saw two young women, also sitting on the slope in meditation.

As I sat there, I kept on being drawn back to the tipi. I could feel a ball of negative energy captured inside. It seemed to be caught in the top third where, I had just been reading, mummification takes place naturally in a pyramid. This energy had a disturbing effect on me, as if a lot of angry talk had been going on in there and was captured. Wondering if there were any other energies running through here, I noticed a large fir tree standing beside the tipis. The fir tree seemed to be transmitting the energy to the hills north of the folk site.

I wandered down and stood beside the empty tipi. On the ground, I could see a silver spiral. Walking along it, I followed it from the doorway to the center, where a small circle of rocks had been placed for a fireplace. Reversing the direction, I walked the spiral out.

Standing outside the empty tipi, I tried to dispel the energy by clapping. At first I felt a bit self-conscious, but then I thought, "What the heck. This is a learning experience." The energy seemed to be held strongly within and I could only think that the energy would dissipate after the tipi had been taken down. I also realized that clapping was something I'd been doing a lot of, lately, in working with energies.

Spirals 9.00 pm

After the fire ceremony had finished, we walked back with the crowd to the festival site. The pavilions started to fill up again as people wandered in for the final performances.

Later, I traced the energy spiral in the gravel at my feet. The line had entered the tipi and spiraled around clockwise and then, when it reached the center, spiraled out anti-clockwise – side by side with the incoming line. As I stood gazing down at the patterns, they reminded me of the yin-yang symbol, and a number that intrigued me – the number 69.

Chapter Nine
The White Warriors

The Rainbow Serpent's Cave
Emails

Hi Brett,

I had a few unusual things happen lately and was wondering if you had any ideas that might throw some light on them. The first part is an on-line conversation with a friend and the second is a vision I had while visiting my parents.

Here's the first part.

DreamSnake: NTA......*S*

NTA: DreamSnake : Howdy

NTA: The energy here is still zooming, giving lots of folks headaches, including me. Be glad when the moon takes a nap.

NTA: Was just thinking "I ain't doing nothing, til they turn the energy down a notch". May just go to the beach. Lol

DreamSnake: So, all these things that are happening is new energy coming in....read about the Kumhb Mela in India....this is the one that they've been waiting for...big Gateway opening~

NTA: Yuppers, lots of new coming in – if the gods don't start fighting over the space ports again. Gold Coast West Africa is next after India

DreamSnake: When will Aus come on line?

NTA: Aus to come on line – don't think they ever went off line. A trip north to the rainbow serpents great caves is where I would look.

NTA: Good Journey Gentle One – enjoy the cool waters of the cave

DreamSnake: thought you'd gone...*S*

NTA: naw, still here, wired to the hilt – energy is bouncing

NTA: those caves are the home of the great painted serpent, the one who touches the skies, keepers, bird people.

NTA: The white painted warriors await you, they know you are coming, and why.

DreamSnake: felt an opening inside last night...very calm and balanced..*S*..a hint to where these caves are

NTA: Arnhem – between the four great directional rivers – at the gateway.

DreamSnake: Physical journeying??..or spirit.

NTA: DreamSnake: Is there a difference? Enjoy

Part 2

I was meditating on a riverbank where I'd once spent a lot of time fishing as a teenager. It was in the middle of the day so I found the shade of a tree on the bank to escape the heat. There was a boat out in the middle with a couple fishing.

Everything went as usual until I was reaching the end of my meditation. Suddenly, it was night and I found myself in the center of a circle of warriors, their entire bodies covered in white ochre, and wearing long white feathered headdresses. (I envied their feathers *Smiles*)

I was compelled to stand up and, with them still circling me, they moved me to the next tree on the riverbank (seemed important) and then I had to climb up the riverbank, walk along the track back to the car, where I hopped in and drove away. As I was negotiating the way out I thought, "Oh, well. Meant to be."

As I walking along the track on the way back, I could change it from bright daylight on the riverbank, to dark night within the circle of warriors. I didn't feel threatened, but was unsure of what it meant. I seem to be focused on the face of a young warrior. I wondered if it was a past life death experience but have no prior recall of living (or dying) there.

I didn't think anything more of it at the time because when these things happen there is often a waiting period before the next event happens, or before an explanation follows.

Since then I have received more information, but would appreciate any light you can put on the subject at this time …

~Blessings and Peace~

INTERPRETING THE WHITE WARRIORS

PART 1 – Your Dreamsnake connection.

The Dreamsnake conversation messages are very confusing, could not make too much sense from them, but will have a go from what I receive on consultation with "you know who".

1. It appears there is much knowledge awakening to be discovered for the Dreamsnake. The White Warriors are messengers of another dimension (spirit world). The white feather parts worry me though – a warning!

Dreamsnake should be careful on how the information is interpreted or used – the right path must be taken for future directions.

2. The Rainbow Serpents Cave and its waters is, I feel, a reference that the receiver should recharge the path of the kundilini, travel the cool cave waters of knowledge to reach or seek the pure knowledge awaiting within the serpents cave pathway or trail. I think this is also telling the receiver that perhaps he (or she) – the inference is someone with feminine attitudes or something – is, may be, or is intending to take, do something or has done something that will lead ultimately along the wrong path.

Knowledge is where you seek it and "north" may mean "beyond the mind," "the extensions beyond leaving the mind". Dreamsnake will enjoy the journey he/she takes and feel refreshed. I don't think it means an earthly direction.

3. The Arnhem reference could be a relationship or ancestral message (see 4 also). Look to the past for the knowledge of the future. Settle down and relax. Be calm. Seek and ye shall find. Your answers to quests proposed by you may lie in the past.

4. The four directional rivers lead to "AR-NUM/AR-NOOM" – travel the first four levels to reach the fifth – the physical gaining of knowledge. On keeping to the

river/cave path of the serpent through the darkness, you shall reach the White Warriors or "The Bird People". These are all Kundilini inferences. These references are also part of "special" Aboriginal "histories". I can say no more.

I don't know if all this makes sense to you – but that is my interpretation from what has been given to me.

PART 2 – Interpreting your other message …

1. This is definitely a warning or premonition! Are you planning or intending to go there at some time in the future? It appears you may intend to meditate at the place of an old tree of which you are unaware is an old Aboriginal ceremonial site or commence meditations aimed at the wrong direction or pathway. Whatever it is, you have or will do something detrimental at this place wherever it is.

2. "Night" means darkness or impending danger. This is the wrong place or pathway. You may through your meditations call upon forces of the dark side. "The Circle" indicates protection of or from. "Warriors covered in white ochre.. feathers etc" are your protectors who have come at that moment. White indicates the position of a "kundiril: Kundiri: Kundi'il" – a spiritual teacher sorcerer – a powerful person. They can be good or bad entities.

3. "Compelled to stand up" – you were being guided/ instructed/ or moved to another safe location/pathway/ direction by these protectors or messengers. There was danger in where you were seated etc. or in what you were doing. The "circle" was protecting you on your way to the safe location/pathway or "tree" attached to a waterway or stream. The tree could also be a Kundilini reference. This may indicate you are heading in the wrong direction or doing something that will lead you to harm and you needed the guidance.

4. When you arrived "at the next tree" still protected by "the circle", you have taken notice and learnt whatever you have to learn. Then you were able to go forward unaided and unprotected by yourself and go into "the world" or other levels of existence.

5. However, as you walked along the track (representing a river or caveway), you persistently changed directions of learning from the ill-advised (dark) to the correct (bright light). "The circle" also indicated a ring of protection by men keeping an eye on you. This also indicated you were taking too many different pathways at the same time and not concentrating on your main pathway of learning or teaching or something. You are being indecisive??

6. Whatever message you received was telling you to be careful in what you do, say or act, or who you associate; they may not be what they present. Choose your paths

carefully spiritually because this appears to be the problem area. Do the right thing or exercise more care when you enter sacred sites or places. Perhaps you've done something or will be tempted to do something you should not. Who knows? These are just possible answers.

7. Finally, the ultimate revelation of which I shall reveal to you. There are two classes of White Warriors. The Spiritual Feathered Messengers of good are called "Kun'diri". They are the spiritual medicine men who always travel in the white bright lights. The White Feathered Warriors who travel the dark sides are called "Kai'daitchi". These "beings" were referred to as "The Bird People". You were apparently visited or given a message from the good messengers – you were privileged!!!

I trust this shows some light upon your divinations and meditory revelations. The above information is given as guidance based on what you have told me from what I am permitted to tell you. Just don't go … unless you are well prepared or in the right frame of mind or intent – that is the message in general tones.

Blessings to you too …. Brett J. (Mira'ji).

The Forest Guardian

The land called Wednesday morning; it'd been a while between visits! With the car parked under the trees beside the creek, I strolled along the creek flats and up the hill to the 'tipi site'. Squatters had once lived on this spot inside a huge tipi, but the site was empty now. Standing on the center of the leveled area, I looked down through the trees and along the energy line that ran towards the front of the land. This energy line had changed – as had all the lines; they were floating, seemingly unstable. The power spots along the lines had also moved, drifting around. I wondered where and when – or if – they would stabilize.

I clambered up the hill through the undergrowth, following the dozer tracks along the ridge and up to where Tree Spirit had bid me farewell. It had become a favorite place to visit, of late. Opening a small collection of crystals, I arranged them in a hollow in the ground beside the apple gum tree, and then sat gazing out across the valley, listening to the hum of the land.

Tree Spirit appeared. He beckoned and turned up the hill. I quickly got up to follow, and then glanced back, unsure, at the crystals. "Should I leave them like this?" I wondered, eyeing them on the ground. Tree Spirit was moving up the rough track left by the bulldozer, a shimmering oval of energy, blurring the natural colors of the forest behind him. I bent down and quickly rearranged the crystals to alleviate the energy, and then stood back, ready to move off. Yet the new arrangement was so glaring to my eyes that I had to put them back the way they were. Tree Spirit was now almost out of view, twenty to thirty steps up the path. Still unhappy with the way the crystals were lying, I left them there and hurried to catch up.

Part One

We climbed towards the top of the hill, the presence of the nature spirit guiding me along a track that appeared before my feet. Between the trees and through the tall grasses we walked, moving higher and higher towards the peak.

A pathway appeared at my left, calling. I paused, looking ahead to where Tree Spirit was in front. I turned, drawn onto the pathway, and followed it for only a few steps when I stopped and laughed. There was a pine tree! And another smaller one was standing right beside it. *Grandfather Tree,* was the thought that came to mind. I placed a friendly hand on the large pine, and looked for a landmark to be able to find this spot again, but the trees were so densely packed that I couldn't see beyond them.

I peered along the narrow clay track as it meandered along the side of the hill, and then glanced up through the trees to where I sensed Tree Spirit was still moving towards the top. Finding my feet taking me further along the track, I followed it in and soon came to a gum tree. It was huge! Inspired by its immensity, I ran my eye up its trunk to where it disappeared into the canopy. Sitting down, I leaned back against it, resting in the shade. It was a peaceful spot, and I fell into meditation.

Before I left, I felt the need to sing a few notes within the aura of this tree, listening as they drifted through the vibrant forest. The pathway continued across the hillside, leading me to another white gum tree. This one was big as well! It wasn't as large as the first one, and it had a different feel to it, gentler and more sensitive. Sitting in the stillness of the bush, I also sang there. Having come across two large gum trees, and with three being a recurring number in my life, I was expectantly looking for the third gum.

A short walk along the animal trail ... and there it was! Another huge gum tree I hadn't met before. I was surprised to find trees of such girth and height still left out here. On an impulse, I wrapped my arms around this tree and lightly kissed its bark before turning round and making my way back along the track. As I passed the other two gum trees, I stopped to hug and then kiss them also.

I stood back on the spot where I'd left Tree Spirit, considering which way to take down to the creek, when I got a strong pull towards the top of the hill. Surprised, I turned towards the summit, out of sight amongst the trees. I wasn't expecting to go there today, but the energy was insistent. As I considered the long, hard climb up the slope, I thought how an image of the sitting rock had come clearly to mind last night in bed, even though there had been no expectation of even visiting out here today.

With a sigh, I began the long walk to the top, slowly winding my way up the hill. It wasn't as difficult as expected; in fact, it was quite easy. The track beneath my feet was warm, almost pulling me up the hill. I had no trouble finding the sitting rock either, perched as it was below the peak. I climbed up onto it, settled myself, and closed my eyes.

Vision at the Four Rivers

I stood gazing across the four rivers from atop a plateau that projected out from the base of a mountain. The sun's rays were peeping over the horizon, golden beams that flickered over the tops of a forest sweeping out below me. Between the trees, thin strips of silver could be seen – the winding arcs of the rivers – reflecting the fading light of the setting sun. The scent of salt drifted upon the evening breeze, a hint of ocean that lay beyond the horizon line. The view was enchanting, and I watched as the last rays of sunlight faded over the darkening forest.

Behind me were a group of warriors, dressed in markings of white clay. Nearby was a circle of rocks. A young warrior approached and stood beside me. He must have known I was captivated by the view for he started moving across my line of vision, breaking my concentration. I turned towards the circle of rocks, aware of him turning with me, and saw the white warriors were making preparations outside the circle.

We moved over to the circle of rocks, this young white warrior and I, to step inside, and together we traced the perimeter of the circle. He seemed to be following me, watching intently. The others were outside, quietly busy, leaving us undisturbed.

It was very dark; something was drawing me. Was that a group of rocks in the center? Squinting down at the ground, I saw, or sensed, a large crystal standing in a ring of small stones.

I walked over to it, and then around it, peering down. The crystal was almost knee high out of the ground, and shaped like a teardrop with the point downwards. It appeared to be dark, as if it was smudged with soil. (Later, I remembered that this crystal had appeared the night before as I was falling asleep.)

I was leaning over, examining it in the dark, when it made contact. The crystal filled my mind, light consumed my body, I was lifted up ... and then just as quickly it withdrew, and I was standing beside the crystal again. Startled, I wondered at what had just happened. The touch of the crystal had filled me in an instant, and I had only been looking at it! I glanced over to the young warrior standing beside me. He was staring intently down at the crystal.

Gently, I reached out with my mind to the crystal. We connected. My presence filled the crystalline teardrop, and again I was absorbed in the light. This time the awareness of self was strong. Then I was back, standing in the circle in the fading twilight, the young warrior beside me unmoving, watching.

Thinking that was the end of the experience, I leaned back into myself, wondering about these connections with the crystal, when my mind was strongly drawn back to it. And then we merged and I forgot everything. The 'I' disappeared; the crystal was in me; I was in the crystal. We were One – joined with each other – combined, in unison.

The group of white warriors were now standing around the outer ring of rocks, and a low chant began.

My consciousness was lifted up to a point directly above the crystal. Pulsating white lines of energy were flowing into this place from different directions.

The lines grew bigger. The point became a spinning sphere of white that grew larger, building and building … until streams of light burst out, flung back along the lines of energy. From my perception in the sphere above the glowing crystal, I was able to follow the lines as they ran outwards.

One energy line flowed southwest to the western-most tip of the continent. One flowed straight down into the red center, and another southeast to the central eastern coast. This energy line met the coast, and then turned southwards. In my mind's eye, I saw it follow the coast down to the south-eastern corner of the continent and suddenly turn eastward, shooting across the Pacific Ocean to pass near, or deviate to, Easter Island, and then onwards into the great mountains of Peru.

One line fled directly north into the Asian peninsula, and another travelled northwest towards India. The last line led northeast through the Pacific islands, and over the ocean to Hawaii. There was a blockage along this line. I tried to clear it by sending Love, but it remained firmly blocked.

I stayed as long as possible in the vision, until I could hold it no longer. And then the link was broken; the warriors wandered away from the circle, and I opened my eyes to the silence of the trees at the top of the hill.

The Ghost People

They are the keeper of old secrets, the ways of the wind …
The distant breezes that blow on my face …
They are hidden in the ways of the ghost people …
The dreams found in the holy smoke …
With the colors that will live forever …
As you reach for the stars of the world …
The ghost people have the knowledge that is the prize
of Mystics …

Who can fly on the breath of the dragon and chase
visions to the future …
This will open the theater of the surreal …
The intimate mysteries of magic …
Here you will see the woman of the smoke who will
touch herself and dissolve into the fog of reality …
As she mixes with your memories, bringing you to the
lost centuries of man …
Her eyes will lead you to the path lined with mirrors …
As you walk into the reflection of your inner being …
Finding the old secrets of the ghost people …
That live in the breezes that blow on my face …

Magicheart 2001

PART

TWO

Contents

Part Two

Chapter One

The Light on the Beach

Sunlight sparkled off the tops of the waves as they gently swept over the golden sands with a soft hiss. Squinting into the morning sun, we gazed over a deep blue ocean basking under a cloudless winter's sky. Taking off our shoes, my wife and I pushed through the deep sand at the end of the boardwalk, and walked down to firmer footing near the water's edge.

Tents lined the sand dunes, and we passed campers and sunbathers enjoying the mild day and calm sea. The sun was warm, but the breeze was cool on our backs as we walked along the edge of the water, out of reach of the breaking waves. Following the curve of the bay around, we'd soon left the sun-seekers and campers behind, and searched for interesting things on the beach. A few shells presented themselves, and some unusual and pretty rocks.

Halfway around the cove, we came across a mound of smooth, colored rocks washed up on the beach. Going with an inner urge, I placed a feather from my hat upright amongst the pebbles. The wind had gained in strength, and the feather fluttered madly in the breeze. I wondered if it'd be there on the way back.

We walked on, and soon had reached the end of the sandy bay where black basalt rocks jutted out into the sea. While my wife wandered off to explore the pools lying amongst the large rocks on the edge of the water, a nicely placed flat rock on the sand beckoned.

I sat down upon it, watching the waves splashing over the volcanic rocks and casting white flecks of foam high into the air. Listening to the sounds of the waves, and with the cool breeze on my face, I closed my eyes in meditation.

Light appeared around the base of the rock; a pool of shining yellow was slowly creeping out over the sands in a circle from the rock. It slowed – and then stopped – a radius of about twenty paces from where I sat, centered in this circle of light. At a point directly behind me, and at the outer edge of this circle, a presence made itself known. It seemed familiar …

This quietly waiting figure drew my attention. Tentatively, I reached out with my mind to where he stood. Recognition came. He seemed younger than before, his face more angular, his body thinner, a small pointed, triangular beard on his chin. His light was more refined, too, yet earthier somehow. Different he appeared – and happier.

I waited expectantly for him to greet me, and when there was no reply, gently sent a welcome. Yet he seem-ed content to maintain his distance on the edge of the circle. Enjoying his presence, the sounds of the ocean, and the warm sun, I dropped back into meditation.

He began to move. Slowly gliding across the sand towards me.

This was unexpected! Startled by his approach, ten-sion rose in the heart. With my eyes still closed, and my inner vision turned towards him, I watched nervously as he came closer and closer ...

He stopped, directly behind me. I tried to keep calm but the tension in my heart quickly grew into panic. Lifting his hands, he slowly reached forward until his fingertips were just above my shoulders. Then his light began to flow into me, streaming in on waves of peace, dissolving the inner tension.

As the light poured into me, the center of my being became a sphere of blossoming light, expanding out in to my body, flowing out into my arms and legs, filling me.

Most radiant was the light in my heart. The sense of 'I' – of identity, of individuality – was still strong, yet I was able to follow his light as it ran deep inside.

I imagined he was now looking out through my eyes, or perhaps he was prompting me, for I opened my eyes to the sunlight reflecting brilliantly off the tops of the foaming waves as they crashed onto the black rocks lining the shore.

Later, as we walked back along the beach, we came to the mound of rocks where the feather had been placed. It was still standing upright on the beach, and fluttering madly in the wind.

Picking up the feather, I held it tightly against the strong breeze, and tried to work it back into the hat-band. I struggled with it several times until a gust of wind whipped the feather out of my hand, and sent it spinning over the sands. I took a few quick steps to-wards it when another gust of wind sent it cartwheeling even further down the beach. Taking the hint, I sent acknowledgement and thanks and turned back into a wind that had suddenly grown cooler, and headed up the beach.

Near the boardwalk, I looked back along the bay. It seemed as if a line had been drawn across the beach. It ran through the mound of rocks, dividing the small sandy bay in half, and I wondered what part the feather had played in it.

After writing this story, it still seemed incomplete. Then, while contemplating how to finish it, this memory (or vision) arose …

When he had stood behind me with his hands on my shoulders, and his essence had flowed deep inside, merging with my light, I was able to follow his light as it had …

Spread out into the world.
Touching everything.
Reaching into everything.

Into the trees and rocks.
Into every person.
And then further out into the stars …

Into every Atom … of every Star.

The Light on the Beach

And I saw that,
He is aware of … his Connection … to All Things.

Then he showed me the People.

And with it came …
Respect for Christianity, and for Buddhists,
For Hindus and Native Americans,
For paganism and nature worshippers –
For within Nature lies the essence of God …

For past Humanity and future offspring,
And for those in strange attire I didn't recognize …

Where is the difference between them?
And I could see no difference.
No Separation.

For We Are All Connected.

Chapter Two

Two Trees

One afternoon, my teenage son and I went for a drive out into the valley. He wanted to visit an old haunt – a creek where catfish lived, and small rainbow-colored fish could be collected for his aquarium. It's a long walk up the creek to the waterholes, but it's a pretty spot and well worth the effort.

Ten minutes short of our destination, as we were traveling along this dusty, winding road, a cattle truck sped round a corner, filling the road in front of us. Hitting the brakes, I quickly pulled up in the long grass on the edge of the road. As the truck thundered past, I saw a long, black figure suddenly shoot out of the grass, right in front of where we'd stopped. Big snake, I thought to myself, but as it moved up onto the verge of the road, I could see it had legs! It was a big, old goanna. If we hadn't pulled up when we did, we'd have driven over him as he lay unseen in the tall grass. They are solid little creatures, and this was a big one! Spontaneously seizing the opportunity, I jumped out of the car and followed him.

I stood looking around. It was very quiet. Where was he? About twenty paces away, I could see a few blades of long grass moving. I started walking quickly towards them, when I saw two black eyes peering at me – and then he was off, weaving his way through the long grass and racing towards two trees standing together in this flat, open, grassy field. These large lizards are fast climbers, and I knew he was heading for safety. He disappeared into the shadows of the trees and I wandered up, intrigued by the glimpses I'd seen of his markings.

There was a very strong vibration as I approached the two trees – a feeling that special energy resided here. It was humbling, and I paused.

Kneeling down, I touched my forehead to the earth, and then leaned back onto my haunches. Both trees were medium sized, standing shoulder to shoulder in an otherwise treeless meadow. *Companion trees*, was the thought that arose. Their branches reached out, gently caressing each other, their leaves throwing a pleasing dappled effect onto the ground. The goanna was noisily scurrying up one of them. My gaze was drawn into the dark shadows under the trees. Slowly standing up, I walked over and ducked under their trailing branches.

It was cool and moist inside, the fallen leaves a soft blanket to walk upon. With the scent of humus and damp soil rising underfoot, I let my eyes adjust to the muted shadows after the bright sunlight of the fields. Filtering down through the thick canopy were thin beams of light, bouncing off the leaves and dancing amongst the shadows. I watched, admiring this play of light and dark, when my eye was caught by the flickering edges where the sunrays and the shadows met. Tiny twirling sparkles appeared on this indefinable edge between shadow and light. I peered quizzically at them, finding myself becoming mesmerized as a gap opened, a space between worlds, and stood transfixed as I was drawn into their realm.

And I was standing in the cool of the trees again, feeling slightly disoriented, the moment slipping away, only to be remembered later while writing. With a mental shake, I realized my son was still waiting in the car. Quickly, I looked around and saw a small branch lying on the ground – a pine branch. It was warm in my hand, and the feel and scent of the wood enhanced the sensation of being under these two powerful and friendly trees. Balancing the branch in my hand, I wondered what to do next.

My eyes were drawn to the other tree – a gum. I quietly stepped up to it, and gently placed a hand on its trunk, and then the other, awkwardly trying to get my footing amongst its gnarled roots, to lean over and place my forehead against its rough bark. It radiated its own aura, yet I could feel its connection with the other tree, and the sense of camaraderie they shared.

With my forehead still pressed against the rough bark, a clawing, scrambling sound could be heard overhead. I looked up through the branches and saw the goanna climbing towards the top of the tree. I'd forgotten about him!

He was pretty big, too, bigger than at first glimpse. I guessed he'd stand shoulder-height from the tip of his tail to the end of his long nose. He was very dark skinned, almost black, with only a few colors visible. I studied him, trying to memorize his markings before he slowly climbed out of sight into the top branches.

Two Trees

The energies were still intense, but I could feel my time here shortening. I moved around under the trees quite happily, but unsure as to the purpose of this visit. Knowing I had to get going soon, I stepped out into the sunlit field and looked around to see if any energy lines were visible.

Different lines radiated out. Two lines from the south seemed to converge on the companion trees. Another line ran away over the flat green fields to trees upon a distant hilltop in the west. On the other side of the road, in the east, was a huge ghost gum. He seemed to be connected with these two trees, but it was confusing. It was as if the energy was spiraling into this big white gum tree, and then merging with other energies before being diverted through the portal of the two trees.

It was with a feeling of dissatisfaction that I left. The trees readily acknowledged my presence at the leaving time, which helped verify the visit, but it felt like something was missing. Perhaps greater illumination would come later in the day.

Chapter Three

Rainbows

It was a flat tyre that did herald our arrival at the creek.

Just as we were driving down the last steep hill, the car began to drag on one side. There was nowhere to stop, so I continued on down, revving the engine to push through the soft sand in the shallow creek, and then up to a grassy spot. There's a lovely feel to this bit of bush and it was good to get out, stretch, and breathe the clean air.

The afternoon passed and we readied to leave. Driving up the hill, we crested the top, and there waiting for us was an acquaintance, Ross. He was obviously curious to see who'd driven along this isolated, dead-end road and past his small farm. We pulled over and spent twenty minutes catching up on local news.

It's an excellent view from the top of the hill. I could see across the open grazing fields for miles, right up to the mouth of the valley where the road passes between two large, rounded hills, standing like sentinels.

In the middle distance, upon the flat grasslands, was a rainbow. Its tall, colored arch shone clearly against a sky of grey and black, for rain clouds were coming in from the east, tipped by golden rays from the lowering sun. There was an impulse to race down and see it, but I knew it would have disappeared by then. It was good to catch up with this local resident, but it was already late afternoon, and with a forty-minute drive still in front of us, I was impatient to go.

We were driving out of the hills at the foot of the mountain range when we glimpsed the rainbow again. Luminous arcs kept appearing and disappearing between the hills as we meandered along the twisting dirt road. It looked enormous in the distance! I kept expecting it to fade, but it stayed firmly in front of us.

The hills gave way to the wide grasslands and there it stood – a huge shining rainbow, towering over us, iridescent against the billowing black clouds, each foot landing in the fields on either side of the road. An unforgettable image.

As we rounded a corner onto a straight section of road, I saw we were heading directly towards the center of this magical arc. Yellow Brick Road?

Rainbows often disappear as they are approached, but this one stayed complete as we drove up to, and then through, its glowing archway, both feet remaining clear and bright. I looked up through the windscreen, watching as it sailed overhead.

Beside me sat my son, between his knees a bucket of water filled with small fish from the creek. He was nursing the bucket to reduce the shock to the fish, so hopefully they'd survive the journey home and live to swim in his fish tank. I was searching my mind for a clue to the meaning of this incredible incident, when the thought arose that this was for my son; in some way it was connected to him. Maybe something had happened while he was down at the creek … I asked, but couldn't hear his reply over the noise of the engine, and when I asked again, he wouldn't say.

Settling back into the drive, and still awed by the experience, I realized that he probably wouldn't remember this, but there would be others for him to know of. Perhaps this one was for me – to let me know that everything was okay – that he was on his path too.

Chapter Four

Who Shot Nelson Mandela?

> *When things get screwed up to a point of severe consequences, the universal consciousness takes over (for the good of all). An overlap or rewrite backs up events and creates another parallel universe, and picks up again. A radio show referenced a good example of this, with many people thinking they remembered Mandela of South Africa's funeral, but he is not dead today.*
>
> *NTA*

When this quote appeared in the review log of a chat room at Spiritweb.org (now defunct), it caught my attention. The first part about the overlap gave me something to think about, but it was the second part – the reference to Mandela – that rang a bell. Yet I couldn't quite put my finger on what it was …

Then one night he came on the television news, smiling and waving to the crowd, and I thought, "How odd they've got him on now that he's dead. Perhaps it's to do with a social program he'd started, and now it's eventuated … or something."

But by the time the film clip had ended, no mention had been made of his recent death. Strange, I thought. Then the cameras returned to the newsreaders and neither face showed any sign of the tragedy having just passed – and when the newsreader said his name there was no tragedy in her voice associated with it either ... and then they moved on to the next item.

I sat stunned for a moment. Had I missed something here? The newspaper! But there was nothing in today's issue. Stranger. Such stories are always followed up, although as it gets older it's usually placed further back in the newspaper. Yet I remembered reading about his death in the café over coffee last week. There'd been a photo on the front page, and the feeling of not being altogether surprised that it'd happened.

So I kept an eye out for it, but nothing appeared in the newspaper the next day, or the day after ... and eventually I forgot about it.

Sometime after this memory had surfaced, I joined an e-mail group. One of the recent threads of conversation was from members who remembered the deaths of famous people – actors, politicians, celebrities – who had then made a reappearance on TV or in the newspapers.

I posted the story up and the responses were interesting. A small number of people remembered him being shot, but oddly enough, no-one else remembered him dying. There were variations on how it had occurred, but all agreed a black African male had been involved.

My wife read this story as I was finishing it, and also remembered him being shot, yet not dying. But, of course, it never happened, did it?

So, do you remember when Nelson Mandela was shot?

Chapter Five

Ball of Light

Just after the shortest day of the year, I was making my way down to the creek with empty buckets in hand, when a light flashed in the sky. I automatically turned towards it and for an instant squinted into the sun, low over the hills in the east.

I blinked from under the brim of my hat … and it was gone! I stared in astonishment and blinked again. The sun had disappeared! One moment I was staring directly at it, and the next moment the sky was empty! Then I remembered that it was afternoon and the sun wouldn't be coming from that direction anyway. Quickly scanning the horizon line over the eastern hills, and seeing no trace of the light, I turned toward the sky and saw the yellow, wintry sun over my left shoulder.

I paused, pondering. I was *sure* I had just looked directly into the sun – yet it couldn't have been. Was it the reflection off a plane? The drone of its engine over the quiet countryside would have alerted me to its presence – and all was silent. A UFO? Perhaps, but it seemed unlikely, although there had been sightings out this way. Nothing more suggested itself and so, with an inner shrug, I continued on my way.

A short distance further down the hill, my attention was again drawn by a flash of light from the east. I cast a glance towards it and, there in the gully, not far from me, was a ball of light, hanging in the air! I stopped and watched while the ball flickered in and out of the sunlight and then slowly faded away. When I looked away from it, the ball reappeared in my peripheral vision. Realizing it was being seen with the inner sight, I picked a grassy spot on the slope and sat down, the empty buckets beside me, and waited quietly as the globe slowly came into view.

It was the size of a basketball and shining with a white radiant light. From my position on the slope, it was just above eye level, about two man-heights off the ground. I watched it for a long while, but it just hung there, silent and unmoving in the air, gleaming softly in the late afternoon light. Deepening my vision brought no new insights. Tired of waiting, and with the afternoon waning, I continued on down to the creek to refill the buckets.

On my return, I was pleased to find it still there. Putting the two buckets of water down on the ground, I settled myself for another wait. There didn't seem to be any change in the glowing ball and I wondered how long it would stay. There was only about an hour of daylight left, judging by where the sun was above the hills behind me. I watched and waited.

The shadows lengthened. I would have to leave for home soon, yet here was this most splendid vision in front of me that didn't make any sense! Deciding to stay a little bit longer, I gathered myself for a final wait.

As the sky darkened, tiny sparkles of light began to appear around the ball. At first, I thought it might have been the last rays of sunlight flickering through the trees, or those little points of white light sometimes seen on the edge of vision. But after the sun had fallen behind the hill and the land lay in shadow, they became brighter, and I realised they were outside of me, rather than across my retina. There was a sense of distance. Some were further away than others and they seemed to be moving in different directions. They would appear – a tiny blaze of white light scudding across the fields – and then disappear, like fast-moving fireflies.

Soon more and more of these points of light appeared, growing brighter against the dimming landscape. It was fascinating and quite beautiful to watch. They reminded me of elves or nymphs, somehow; light-hearted and free was the inner impression. I tried to see where these specks were coming from, but this was difficult to determine, for they were moving so quickly, zipping past, appearing and disappearing in an instant.

I finally caught a speck as it flashed by, following it with my eyes, and was startled when its flight was interrupted by the ball of light. It had simply sped into it and vanished!

Focusing my gaze on the ball of light, I saw other specks flying in from different directions. They would zoom in and crash into the ball, and as each speck hit, a little flash of light would erupt on the ball's surface.

The twilight deepened; the ball's soft radiance grew brighter. Evening was closing in but I was hesitant to leave. Should I go yet? How long would the ball of light linger? Would it still be here the next time I was out?

I stood up, trying to decide whether to clean up before nightfall or sit down again, when the ball began to move, almost imperceptibly at first. I stared hard at it. Then, against the slope of the hill behind, I could see that the ball was indeed moving.

It began to slowly float down along the gully. I stood rooted to the spot, watching as it silently drifted onto the creek flats and wondering whether I should try to follow it. The ball of light started to pick up speed. As it followed the pathway along the creek, it got faster. It would take a quick trot to keep up with it now. Before I could make a decision whether to chase after it or not, it seemed to shoot off. In a flash, it was zooming along the creek flats towards the front of the land. It would be out of sight in a moment. There was no way to run after it now!

Anxiety arose. "Surely there is more to it than this," I thought desperately, as it disappeared into the gathering gloom. "Nothing has happened, and now it's leaving!"

And then my mind became linked with it, and I was able to follow the ball's progress as it swung around the curve of the creek and hurtled towards the gate. My perception began to flow along this link and, suddenly, I was sitting atop the ball.

It sped through the twilight, shining softly beneath me. It was exhilarating watching the trees lining the creek sweep past from a view above head-height. It certainly gave a different perspective on familiar landmarks!

We neared the campsite at the creek, flying through the darkness together. Beginning to wonder where it would go when it reached the road, the ball swerved sharply just before the gate, and spun around the hill at the front of the land.

My perception changed; I was left standing beside the gate, yet still connected to the ball along the mind link.

I followed it as it raced along the ridge towards the back of the land, and then shot across to the hill on the neighboring property. Sweeping up the steep slope, it stopped at the summit. The ball of light seemed to 'arrive' at this spot. It felt comfortable there, like it had come home. (Did it go through a gate?) Another intelligence was also there – a greater intelligence – and a transference of energies took place. Dialogue, or data, was being exchanged.

What was happening, I wondered?

By focusing inward, impressions arose. Those tiny specks of light came to mind. Sitting on the slope, and watching them zip into the ball, I remembered how they'd been flying in straight lines from different places on the land. And I realized that each particle had carried a separate and distinct energy signature. Mentally tracing one of these particles back to its origin, I saw it'd come from a place where a lot of time had been spent on the land – working and meditating.

Were these energy signatures the vibrations I'd impressed upon the land? Maybe the ball of light was like a report card! Would I pass? Would I get good grades?

Later, as I was writing this story, thoughts began to arise.
They flowed like this …

Memory ceases to exist – living in the Now.
There is no Past – to compare – the Present to.
And therefore, no (potential) Future.

This leads to …
The end of Judgement?
The End of Duality??

Chapter Six

Colors in a Ball

Sitting in the sun by the creek one winter's morning, I was slowly drifting into meditation, when a bright ball of light suddenly appeared. With eyes wide and all thoughts of meditation gone, I looked on in amazement as it swung through the air and stopped right in front of me, hovering in the center of my vision. The surprise was complete, for all thoughts stopped!

After the initial surprise had subsided, and seeing that it wasn't going to disappear as quickly as it had arrived, I looked at it more closely. It was quite simply white, round and glowing, as large as a basketball, and level with my eyes. It appeared to gently sway in the air – as if trying to get my attention. It didn't need to try by now!

With my eyes glued to this ball of light, the greens and browns of the shadowed creek blurred together behind it. Was this the third eye?

As I stared at it in wonder, the mind began to work, searching the memory banks for a clue, for some kind of background to reference this event against. But everything drew a blank.

A thought started to rise. And then stopped. It started to rise. And again it stopped. This irritation drew my attention; I turned to see what it was. A little bubble of consciousness was bouncing off an invisible ceiling.

I delved down to bring this bubble forward, but couldn't quite grasp it. Each time I tried, it slipped away; and then I saw that a force was suppressing it. When the thought arose, this force – the invisible ceiling – would gently, but firmly, stop the bubble from surfacing into consciousness. I knew that this bubble would shed light on what was happening, yet also realized that, for reasons unclear at the time, this knowledge was being deliberately suppressed. Unable to grasp the thought, or allay the force, I let it go. Analysis could come later.

My eyes grew tired from watching the ball. It hadn't moved or changed in appearance. After its sudden arrival, I'd been expecting it to race off at any moment, or for something unusual to happen, but the ball just hung there, glowing silently in the air. I glanced away – when something flashed across its surface.

Quickly, I looked back. The ball was unchanged – glowing, steady, silent. I searched its face, certain I'd glimpsed something out of the corner of my eye. Nothing moved upon its surface.

I was drifting off again when another image raced across the ball … and then just as suddenly disappeared. There'd definitely been something there on the ball's face, and whatever it was, it'd moved fast! With my attention now fixed firmly on the ball of light, I waited with hurried patience.

Another image appeared on the ball's surface, sped across the face, and then vanished. It was hard to tell what it was because it'd moved so rapidly, but it looked like a dark smudge had swept across the ball before disappearing.

Gazing steadily at the ball, I waited to glimpse more. A smudge appeared … and was gone. Another smudge flashed past. I darted my eyes towards it but it had disappeared before I could catch it in my vision. I sat attentively, waiting. More smudges appeared, popping out at random on the face of the ball and vanishing just as quickly. I looked from one to the other, my eyes darting back and forth.

I was growing frustrated. I couldn't see anything. Before I could catch a smudge, it had disappeared. I tried again, widening my vision and focusing harder. Smudges were now appearing all over the face of the ball. I tried to increase my mental speed, but still wasn't able to catch any of these scurrying smudges. Unsure what else to do, I decided to pause for a moment, and relax back into meditation.

I started withdrawing towards the inner world, the ball hovering in the air before me. Through eyelashes, these smudges looked like dark comets racing across the sun. I relaxed further inward. One of the leaping smudges caught my half-open eyes. I glanced at it, to find that not only had I finally caught one of these smudges – but that it was brightly colored – green! Another smudge leapt across the ball. It, too, had taken on a color – red. Now others were also taking on colors!

A blue one appeared, and then a yellow. I opened my eyes wider in curiosity, and the smudges diminished back to their original grey hue, zipping past too quickly to catch. Half-closing my eyes, I slowed the mind and breath, letting the ball float in front of me. The smudges started to appear again in color. I gently opened my eyes a little wider, so that the ball was in focus, and the colors remained steady.

I found that by staring at the center of the ball of light, I could see the smudges more clearly on the edge of my vision, rather than trying to follow them with my eyes. They were all brilliantly colored, and they weren't really smudges at all. As my vision became more acute, I saw they were more of a thick line, with a bulbous head and a disintegrating tail. They would randomly appear on the surface, scud across for a short distance and, before they had reached the edge of the ball, vanish back inside.

A green line drew my attention as it flashed across the ball. It seemed to slow – or my vision was able to focus on it more clearly – for I could see it in greater detail. It was luminous green, broad and short, with a tapering comet-like tail. And then it was gone, disappearing back into the ball of light.

A red line sped past. It slowed, and almost seemed to stop for an moment. My gaze zoomed down on to and I saw, in vivid detail, large, red, crystalline patterns shining on its body. I was drawn up towards its head where a group of sparkling lights shone in brilliant over-lapping designs, ranging from a rich pink to a dark red. And then the line eased past, and was gone.

The ball began to grow bigger, the background of the creek receding until the circle of white light filled my vision. The lines also grew bigger and seemed to move more slowly, allowing me to follow them in closer detail. Intrigued, I watched the colored lines as they flashed across the ball's face.

A blue line sped along the bottom. A yellow line zipped diagonally up across the center. I caught a green line as it emerged, drawing itself out of the ball. It raced across the surface, growing larger as it slowed. As it began to dive down inside the ball, my attention was caught up with it and I could follow it as it pierced the surface. Down it dived, twisting and turning, to find myself sitting on its shoulder. We swept along a green tunnel, spinning and spiraling inside the white ball. It was a wild and thrilling ride.

The walls of the green tunnel began to fade. I saw other colors following their own tunnels of intent inside the ball, ducking and weaving, and leaving after-images in their wake. A red line came spinning towards us and I realized I could change rides! With a burst of exhil-aration, I jumped across, to land atop this red line as it sped past. We raced madly round and round inside the ball, to emerge onto the surface, and then plunge back inside again.

As the ride continued, I noticed that the other lines were changing. Their colors were becoming softer, more mist-like. The tunnels they were following became larger and larger, until they filled the inside of the ball. These colored lines dived and dashed about in a frantic race, yet never crashed into another, or lost their individuality. A joyous dance.

Something started niggling in the back of my mind; there was something I needed to do. I forced my mind to think. What was this ball of light? What did all this mean? The idea came that each color was a dimension. And all the colors were contained within this ball. A dimensional doorway!?

I considered this for a moment, the journey forgotten. Remembering that there may be a guardian, I sent greetings and a mental offering. An image arose in my mind, and the light increased as a sense of acknowledgement, and then contentedness, washed over me. I paused in gratitude, absorbing the feeling for later reflection.

Then the Ball beckoned. "Come," it seemed to say, "Enter."

Yet, I hesitated, thinking, "Where to go? Where do I start? There's so much to see.

"Oh, to be a tourist," I thought longingly. "How long would it take before the wonders of the multiverse paled? A lifetime … many lifetimes!"

Finally, hesitating no longer, I plunged in.

I was standing in space. Myriad pinpoints of light surrounded me, layer upon layer of stars, stretching far back into the inky blackness. Drawing my gaze in closer I saw suns, planets, comets and other luminous bodies sailing past in glorious color.

A massive yellow sun swung by with planets swiftly whirling in orbit. The star quickly grew larger until I was hovering just above its surface, and watched entranced as whirlpools of fire spun and swept across its placid yellow face.

Another star drew near – a vibrant, blazing, red sun – and saw a raging flare whip joyously across its fiery exterior. I gazed upon other stars as they loomed in close, to swing out again and disappear into the heavens.

The thought arose that each star was unique – each had its own particular color, its own individual dance through space, and its own separate and distinct personality. For in that moment, more than just their appearances were revealed. By focusing on a star, its history and development could be read – the evolution of an intelligent awareness.

Planets were also visible, standing out readily to greet me. They were individuals as well, radiating goodwill and intelligence. A small red planet with yellow swirls swooped past, hailing me and revealing information about itself. I followed its flight path against the backdrop of stars and saw other planets in this solar system, each unique, each with their own individual stamp. A huge Jupiter-type planet caught my attention, exuding intelligence and knowing. A tiny blue and white planet swept into view. This one was almost joyful compared to the somber timbre of its larger neighbor.

Overlaying this star scene were the colours of the dimensions, slowly fading and changing. A blue shimmer passed before me, fading into a green one that faded into yellow ... The colors of the rainbow were slowly being superimposed over the stars. I let my eyes absorb this overlay effect of the bright stars shining through the changing, misty colors.

Then the dimensions called. But where to go? A friend had come from the blue universe and, since emissaries had also arrived recently from there, decided to visit it first.

Gazing at the blue stream drew me into its realm, and soon I was hurtling down a space corridor with the colors of the dimensional doorway receding behind me. With the stars whipping past, I focused on where my friend's home was in this universe.

At first I enjoyed the sensation of traveling – like a cool breeze in the face – and of watching the stars slip by. But my attention began to wander. Lethargy arose. I could feel the energy starting to drain out of me and began to wonder if I'd have enough energy to reach my destination.

I came to a halt in space, knowing I was heading in the wrong direction – hence the energy drain – to suddenly realize that my time in the dimensions was limited! I looked around for a new direction. Nothing drew me. The stars seemed distant and dim. Desperation began to rise. I needed to do something quickly before the energy waned even further. This short journey into the blue universe had tired me!

Perhaps this desperation helped me focus, for I relaxed, letting the pressure go. The rainbow colors of the multiverse appeared before me again, drifting in space. Leaning into the colors, I let curiosity and intent draw me …

I fell, spiraling through the dimensions. With a sense of freedom and vertigo, I spun through the reds and yellows, the greens and blues, bathing in the vibrant colors. The heartstrings were being tugged. I stopped and looked behind. A broad, green line was racing towards me. With relief and gratitude, I watched as it neared, its tail echoing into infinity. And then we were joined and I was sitting upon its shoulder once more, soaring through space. We raced towards the green universe and plunged through the veil.

A thick green fog surrounded me. All visibility disappeared. No stars shone; nothing could be seen except this green fluorescent mist. I looked down at it. It didn't cling to me, but it did give me an uncomfortable feeling. There was a vague sense of movement, yet I felt like I was creeping through this vapid atmosphere. How long would it linger? Then, with a great rush, I burst out into a huge star-studded sky.

A sense of well-being instantly arose. I stood gazing happily around at this strange new universe. The stars shone calmly around me.

Now, I thought after a pause, where was I to go in this universe? With that thought, a planet appeared, speeding out of the vastness of black space to meet me. It neared, and I wondered what this planet was called.

"Sara/Tara," a voice said, and standing beside me was an entity in glowing white, with the face and beard of an older man. Although I was startled by his sudden appearance, the voyage continued unabated, the planet sweeping into view. Either this entity had been there all the time, unseen, or had arrived to answer my question.

We came to a halt above the planet's surface and I looked down in wonder. A beautiful rich-green world lay below. As I swung my gaze back and forth across its surface, my vision zoomed down to see massive vegetation covering the planet. Huge trees with enormous boles stood shoulder to shoulder in forests that covered continents. Wild streams twisted their way down steep tree-clad mountains, cutting dark brown paths through the verdant canopy. Newer forests, with smaller, younger trees could be seen on the lower lands, some bordered by lakes and rivers, the only glimmer of blue to be seen. It appeared to be a world of greens and browns, of trees and land, where the essence of vegetation and earth was strong. Nowhere did I find the evidence of people or of civilisation, yet I sensed it wasn't a world uninhabited.

With the entity standing beside me in space, I grew impatient to get closer.

And then I was sitting by the creek again, wrapped in my brown tasseled meditation blanket, the colors of the creek before me, and the sun hot on my back.

Chapter Seven

Dreamsnakes

"Vaporizing clouds is easy enough," I thought, "but how do I make them bigger?" I concentrated on trying to puff up the white fluffy clouds that were rolling over the hills from the west but, if anything, they seemed to be shrinking.

I was sitting comfortably ensconced on a grassy spot among the grasstrees at the bottom of the ridge, looking over an open field that sloped down to the creek flats. It was warm sitting in the sun, protected from the winter's breezes by the tall grasses around me. From my position above the sloping field, I could gaze over the wall of lantana edging the creek flats and down into the trees of the creek. Thoughts began to turn inwards and, with eyes half-closed, looking up at the fluffy white clouds on the horizon, I began drifting into meditation.

Lines of energy began to swim before my eyes. They looked like tiny pieces of glowing white rope, undulating up and down. Each would only last an instant, appearing and then disappearing. A curious phenomenon, I thought, as I watched these shining energy lines flitting across my inner vision. Eventually tiring of their repetitious movements, I struggled to fall back into meditation.

At one point, with the undulating lines still flashing before me, I opened my eyes. Below me was a pathway that ran parallel with the slope. Strange white lines were bobbing along it amongst the tall grasses. They looked like headless snakes that wriggled up and down – rather than from side to side as snakes normally do – and they were moving along the pathway away from me. I squinted my eyes against the bright sunlight, not really believing what I saw. Were they larger versions of the white lines that had been floating across my eyes? There were perhaps half a dozen of these shining snakes, following each other nose-to-tail, and the realization came that they must be moving along an energy line. The pathway followed an energy line!

From my stomach region, I could feel energy being drawn out of me. The further away these headless snakes moved, the greater the draw became. Sensing they were somehow connected to me, I sent a call through the ground to draw them back. They hesitated, and slowed. I called again, watching hopefully as they turned and began to come back along the path, but then they stopped and gathered where two pathways cross, refusing to come any closer. I watched their writhing dance as the winter sunlight flooded down upon the open field. With the energy drain eased, I stood up and, with a great deal of curiosity, began to walk along the path in their direction, my eye upon them.

As I walked along the narrow trail that separated the tall grasses, I could feel the earth under my feet. A warm stream of energy was flowing underneath the pathway, moving up into my legs and almost drawing me along. I stopped on the dirt track, feeling this tingling warmth rising into my body, and watching the shining white snakes twisting upon each other.

My attention was drawn down to the energy flowing beneath my feet. I could follow it with my mind as it ran along this pathway, past where the snakes were tumbling together, and wound its way towards the front of the land. As it neared the creek, it arrowed down towards the circle of rocks at the campsite, crossed the water, and then faded on the hillside opposite.

I neared the energy snakes, still twisting and turning in a huddle where the two pathways met. They weren't holding my attention now and so released them from my mind. They quickly hurried off, once again forming an undulating line nose-to-tail, and disappeared along the track.

I wandered along slowly behind, pausing often to enjoy the view from the hillside and absorb the energies. A little spot amongst the trees called. I dropped down off the track and sat on a grassed area, surrounded by wonderful tree energies. Gazing down into the creek, I fell into the stillness.

Dusk was descending by the time I'd made my way down to the creek and arrived back at the campsite. It was murky under the trees now that the sun had fallen behind the mountains. Standing beside the circle of rocks, I looked along the energy line where it crossed the water and ran up the hillside. Through a gap in the trees, I could see the place on the hill I had just visited.

The week before, I'd been standing by the creek when the strong desire to walk up there had arisen. Unable to resist, I had wandered up, drawn to a log lying about one third of the way up the steep hill. Beside it had been a pile of tumbled and broken rocks, perhaps heaped together by a bulldozer that had made a rough track nearby. Scattered among the rocks were large lumps of quartz crystals, and I had rested there, sitting on the log.

It was very pleasant under the trees in the gathering twilight, and I lingered near the rocks of the camp circle, enjoying the energies. The small flying insects were few at this time of the year and the cool air was yet to settle.

A light drew my attention. Something was shining near a tree on the edge of the camp circle. Yet, I felt no rush to investigate, happy just to watch the last of the daylight fade. An image began forming beside the tree, but still I lingered, gazing over the silent hillside. The clouds above the mountain in the western sky were tipped in pink and purple, and the first stars were twinkling prettily overhead. Then the whitish grasses on the hillside across the creek caught a final glimpse of the fading sun, and for a few moments the grasses glowed as with an inner radiance, before quickly ebbing away.

Taking a deep breath of the cool scented air, I turned towards the faint light glimmering near the tree. It'd grown brighter now amidst the deepening twilight. I stepped through a gap in the circle of rocks and looked down at this glowing oval of misty white light, standing about waist high beside the tree. Moving over closer, I opened my palms, pausing ... The energies were friendly and clear. Placing a hand on the tree, I bent down and stepped into the light.

Part Two

It was soothing standing within the oval light, but I soon tired of my awkward pose. The tree arched over directly above me and I had to hunch down to keep both feet within the light. As soon as I straightened, the curve of the tree would strike me in the middle of the back – I could feel the bark's rough texture through my shirt – and push me forward again. By bending over and bracing myself with my hands on my knees, I could maintain my stance within the oval of light.

Twisting my head to peer around the tree trunk, I looked along the energy line as it ran through the grassy fields of the hillside opposite, past the log and pile of rocks, and disappeared through an opening between the trees higher up.

As I stood there, hunched down in the oval light, and trying to maintain my position under the curve of the tree, a large energy snake began slowly easing itself out of my body. I stared in baffled wonderment it as it flowed out from around the solar plexus region. *Man-sized* is what came to mind. When its full length had left my body, the snake headed down the creek bank towards the water. Glowing white in the dim twilight, as long as I was, and undulating like the smaller energy snakes, it crossed the creek and began following the energy trail through the grassy field and up the hill. Was it a conglomeration of the many smaller energy snakes?

As it moved away, I began to feel uneasy. It was still clearly visible, shining white in the gathering gloom, but the further away it moved, the greater the anxiety became. Earlier, when the smaller energy snakes had moved along the pathway away from me, energy had been drawn from my middle. What would happen this time, I wondered, with so large an energy snake?

I decided to call it back. I sent a message marked "Urgent" along the energy line. And when there was no reply, sent another after it. For a moment, I thought it hadn't heard, but then the energy snake hesitated, and stopped, and then suddenly reared back, fighting against the command. A tussle ensued. I sent another command – an order, a plea – along the energy line. It turned, to draw near the other side of the creek, but wouldn't cross it. Like a frisky dog let off from its leash, it wouldn't quite come within catching distance.

So, with allowing in my heart, I let it continue. It moved off steadily once more, cutting through the grasses and up past the pile of rocks, undulating along the energy line. I watched until its glowing form had disappeared out of sight under the thick trees higher up the hill.

The night grew dark. I stood up, cramped from my position, wondering about, and in wonder of, what had just happened. There was no desire to leave for home just yet. I felt settled and comfortable now, wanting to linger in the energies a little while longer. I glanced around the campsite. The fire circle looked inviting. Gathering twigs and dry leaves, I soon had a small fire going. The flickering flames lit up the overhanging branches, throwing a red cocoon over the campsite. I sat on the large creek rocks of the circle, enjoying the warmth of the fire, and the stillness of the night.

Chapter Eight

Reflection

Earlier in the year, Brett had taken a group to an old aboriginal site where cliffs had once been adorned with paintings, and a shaman's cave. He had been researching the diaries of his great-grandfather, one of the first settlers to this area. Having saved a young aboriginal boy from rushing floodwaters, Brett's forefather had been welcomed, and then initiated, into the tribe. The dairies recorded not only his exploration of this country but also his travels with the boy, Dhakkanguini, who in later years taught him much about the customs and spiritual traditions of his people.

Leading us towards the coast, Brett had turned off the asphalt road and we'd followed each other's dust up a steep, winding, dirt road. The road had leveled out and we'd driven across the top of a plateau, past a few houses and through cow fields, to a picnic area with a superb view.

We had gazed eastwards, down to where farmhouses stood at the bottom of the plateau, vivid in detail and looking fairylike in the clear air. Beyond the farms a massive pine forest swept out, a green canopy that covered this low lying plain. In the central foreground, amidst the forest, was a large loaf-shaped hill that'd once stood on the shores of an ancient ocean. This ocean had also surrounded the plateau, turning it into an island.

To the southeast lay the present ocean, faint streaks of white appearing and disappearing on its troubled surface. The deep blue of ocean had faded into a hazy horizon line of pale blues and grays, meeting and merging with a crystalline winter's sky. With a cool and invigorating air on my face, I had followed the line of the sky as it swept back over us. Further south were the remains of three volcanoes, old mountain friends, and features of this coastal plain. Behind the picnic area was a forestry tower, a tall, thin, white structure rising up out of the cow field.

After lunch, the group had driven back across the plateau to where the road begins to descend. Parking on the side of the road, we'd tramped in through the long grass and investigated the cliffs and cave, the faded relics of the past peoples who had once lived here. Later, as the group had slowly wound its way out of the stone-littered forest and back to the road, something had caught my eye off the track. Barely hesitating, I'd left the line and scampered down the hillside. Hidden amongst the leaves was a little container. Curiously I'd picked it up. It was a small plastic bottle with a metal screw-cap lid. After a hard twist, the lid released, and inside I found white paint filling a third of the jar. And even more surprisingly, the paint had been still moist.

It was the other side of winter when I drove up the narrow, graveled dirt road to the plateau. Today was a day to go exploring by myself. As I climbed, I kept getting the impulse to stop before I reached the top and meditate. I was intending to do a meditation at the picnic spot anyway, and so ignored it, but the niggling grew insistent.

Passing the cliffs on my left, I drove on to the plateau and saw a little clearing to my right. Quickly, I pulled in and parked. A farmhouse stood a short way down the road. I was unsure if this clearing was private property, but I had taken the hint and now began looking for a place to meditate.

Between the trees lining the plateau was a huge view that faced westwards. I walked over to where great slabs of rock jutted out over the edge and sat down on one, gazing across a wide valley of forests and fields to where a line of purple hills rolled away into the distance. The sunlight streamed through the trees, warming the area where I sat.

I had barely settled myself when I heard the caves beneath me calling. Determined to meditate, I kept my eyes firmly closed, yet the energy kept tugging at me. Giving into the pull, I scrambled down the side of the hill, following an animal trail between the large rocks and undergrowth.

These huge rock slabs were stacked upon each other below where I'd been sitting, and the weather had caused indentations in them. Some of these indentations were quite large. One 'cave' had the most pleasant and welcoming feel to it. I wandered along the ledges, enjoying the presence of the caves until I felt it was time to leave.

A pathway led up the hillside. Walking back along the road, I noticed a sign nailed to a tree near where the car was parked, *Private Property – Keep Out.* Smiling to myself, I saw a green and yellow snake had been painted across the top of the sign.

I drove across the top of the plateau and parked at the picnic area beside the remains of two trees. These two trees had once been sacred to the aborigines, and both had been hit by lightning only a few years earlier. The stump remained of one, and the other, while still standing, was also dead. It towered overhead; its branches, bereft of leaves or bark, hung naked against a deep winter's sky. The stump had been used as firewood for a campfire nearby, so little of it remained, but I did manage to collect some of the soft inner wood.

I turned my gaze out from the plateau and down to the farms below. The houses, sheds, fences and tractors all stood out in stunning detail under the bright sunlight. I ran my eye across the dark rich green of pine forests and up to an ocean that blazed out across the horizon.

Wondering where to meditate, I looked around the picnic area. Apart from the small shelter standing in the middle of the deep lawn, it was flat, grassy and open. There wasn't anywhere secluded to sit. I wandered over to the barbed wire fence that ran along the edge of the plateau, separating the picnic area from the pastures. The hill dropped steeply away. A short walk down the side of the plateau would leave me unseen, and un-disturbed, from any new arrivals, I thought.

I eased my way through the strands of barbed wire, and meandered down a stony cow track, cut deep in the thick grass. The air had a crispness to it that made me stop and breathe, letting the tension flow out with the breath. It was calming, yet refreshing.

Below me, the hillside swept down to a semicircle of flat land that jutted out from the plateau. Upon it stood the remains of a circle of trees. There were gaps in the circle but one large gum tree captured my atten-tion. It was dead; its bleached white form standing out vividly against the backdrop of green pine forest, but it had kept its shape.

Although it was a long way down to the circle of trees, I began to eagerly wonder if this was why I was here today – to explore the energies of that site. Large, squarish rocks were scattered on the hillside about halfway down. It looked like a good place to meditate before venturing further on to the circle.

As I slowly wandered down the hillside, the colors of the fields, trees and sky began to glow, shining with an inner light. These colors grew richer and deeper, becoming luminescent, until the landscape was blurred by their radiance.

I stopped and watched as tiny green molecules rose up from the grassy fields and into the air, joining joy-fully together and swirling like a breeze. Behind me, the browns of the forest on top of the plateau were flowing down the hillside, merging with the rising colors of the grass. From above, a blue mist drifted softly down, blending with the swirling greens and browns.

These living colors rolled down the hill to greet me, tumbling waves of luminous light that washed over me, and through me. I stood still, drinking in the vibrant colors, feeling them enter into me, and breathing them deeply into my body. Turning towards the circle of trees, I made my way down towards the sitting rocks, each slow footstep a communion in the colors.

Standing before one of these welcoming, large, flat-topped rocks, I took off my shoes and climbed up on to it. With a cool breeze wafting into my face, I rested my gaze on the loaf-shaped hill rising up from the plain below and half-closed my eyes to meditate. It was peaceful sitting there on the hillside, absorbing the magnetic essence of the colors under my eyelashes as they swirled blissfully around me on the hillside.

Out of the corner of my eye, I caught a glimpse of someone approaching. Startled, I turned round to see a person walking towards me. Worried that I may have been intruding, and concerned that this experience might be interrupted, I was instantly relieved to see the hillside through this shadowy figure.

The dark shape walked up and stopped about five paces away to my left, and slightly behind me. My gaze slid up the tall figure, now appearing more solid. He was wearing dark shoes, blue jeans and a navy-blue shirt – the same clothes as I was! Hesitantly, yet irresistibly drawn, I brought my gaze slowly upwards ... The fair hair that crowned his head was instantly recognizable.

It was me! Dressed in exactly the same clothes – and looking exactly the same!

I regarded him intently to see what he would do next. He was staring across me into the distance, as if watching something and, seemingly, unaware of me. I looked to my right, following his line of vision. The fields ran down the slope to disappear over the edge of the plateau – there was nothing that caught my attention. The line I was following flowed down the hill to the circle of trees. I looked back the way he had come. It ran across the fields to the thick forest that covered the top of the plateau. Was the picnic area in a different place in the world he inhabited?

As I kept my position on the rock, watching at him out of the corners of my eye with my head tilted slightly in his direction, there was a feeling that arose, an essence that connected, an underlying knowing – He was Me.

Would he talk to me, I wondered? Would he tell me about his life? Would I be able to see, and compare, the differences? I waited. He didn't move.

Without physically trying to distract him, I tried to get his attention. I used every trick I could think of, yet still he didn't move. And oddly enough, during the entire time I sat on the rock, neither did I.

Finally, I stood up. He was immobile. I took a few small steps, looked back at him, and awkwardly took a few more. He walked forward. I began to get my rhythm as I moved off down the track. I saw him walking across my path behind me, and then forgot about him as a sense of peace and ease of movement settled over me.

Down, I happily tramped towards the circle of trees, following the winding cow track carved into the green pasture, when I remembered him. I looked around. He wasn't anywhere to be seen. As I scanned the fields, I glimpsed a dark blue shirt floating beside me. I half-turned, looking down at this shadow that moved as I moved, to realize it was his shirt I was seeing. He was with me! We had merged, and were sharing the same space and time together.

I fell back into the moment, forgetting time, forgetting space, enjoying the freedom and peace that came from just being here, now. Together, we moved down the hill.

There came a moment of unease, of inner disruption. I stopped, wondering what was causing these ripples of disquiet. And the thought arose that it was time for my new friend to leave. I started walking again, but the peace was disturbed, the unease continuing. Then he stepped out of me, walking away to my right. I stopped and watched as he moved away at a steady pace, following his original line across the hill.

I waited for him to acknowledge this parting, but he kept on walking. Disappointed, I thought about making my way further down the path, yet I couldn't take my eyes off him. Then he stopped, turned, and looked back along the line he had been following. Just as I was sadly thinking he couldn't see me, he brought his gaze onto me and looked directly at me. And his eyes began to shine. Then he turned and walked away again over the lush green fields.

Part Two

I stood unmoving, watching his dark-dressed figure retreat into the distance. As he reached the curve of the hill and began to drop from sight, he started to flicker in and out of vision, and then vanished.

Chapter Nine

Walkabout

Meher Baba's House
Friday Afternoon

It's a magnificent view from the back of Meher Baba's house. I ran my eye down the side of the mountain as it dropped sharply away to the coastal plains far below, where velvet-green forests sweep away to meet with a deep blue ocean. Cleared patches of land, and roads snaking through the forest, showed the hand of human intervention. Tiny white matchsticks could be seen standing where the land meets the ocean – they were the high-rise buildings at the coastal resorts.

I wasn't sure what had drawn me here today but, while driving past, an image had arisen of a view, fresh air and sunshine. Behind me, a short distance away, was a hilltop crowned in trees. There hadn't been the opportunity to explore there in previous visits and now I was suddenly keen.

A two-wheel track ran level with the hill, cutting through the lawn. It didn't go in the direction of the hilltop but I was irresistibly drawn to walk it. I looked longingly up the hill's side to the unseen peak, but turned and calmly followed the energy flowing along the tracks, gazing out over the panoramic view and feeling the cool ocean air on my face.

Part Two

The light changed. A golden essence descended; the trees and the thick green grass became vibrant and alive, their colors glowing with vitality. My paces slowed as I noted the uniqueness of every tree, how each shone with its own individual spirit, and its own personality and awareness.

The golden light deepened as I walked along the track, as if an invisible line had been crossed. I stopped and walked back a few paces. The light diminished. I took a few steps forward and again it increased. I peered back to where I imagined the line began on the path, and then turned, strolling along in the golden light.

A glimmering shape appeared beside me. It was a short man with dark hair, dressed in a swirling robe and, I thought, with an unusual facial appearance. He became more solid, and as we walked together, he looked up at me and began to talk earnestly. I had no idea what he was saying. I tried, but couldn't concentrate on his words. Whether he was talking in another language, or because my mind was absorbed in the light, I can't say.

He paused, his eyes looking intently, almost fiercely at me, and began to talk again. I realized he was repeating what he had just said. Still, I couldn't make sense of his words. Mentally leaning into his aura, I gently assured him that I was here with peaceful intentions. This seemed to satisfy him and he suddenly left, vanishing. I continued sauntering along the path, wondering about this curious event, yet unconcerned. I was feeling light-hearted and carefree, intoxicated by the golden aura that flooded the landscape.

Another figure appeared beside the path, flickering in the shadows between the trees. This figure was instantly recognizable. It was Meher Baba, dressed in a gown of shining white. As soon as I recognized him, he solidified and, with a radiant smile, came over and joined me. We strolled leisurely along the path. He seemed to be listening intently, looking up at me – perhaps waiting for me to speak – but I was lost in the bliss of the moment, happy to be in his company again.

The pathway came to a bend. It turned and climbed up the hill in the direction of the top. I had been on the right track all along! Together we slowly climbed the hill, passing the tall pine trees that lined the path.

At the top of the hill was a level area surrounded by trees. In the center of this flat spot was a series of large stones spaced out evenly in a circle. I was surprised when I saw them, yet the feeling quickly gave way to pleasure as I ran my eye over them. They looked just right.

Hesitating before the large rocks, I waited for Meher Baba to walk into the circle first, but he paused too, standing just behind me. Unsure, I slowly walked forward, and then he joined me and together we entered the circle of stones.

The energy was stronger within the circle – clearer, finer, like a still pool of white light. I moved to the center and slowly spun round, gazing out through the trees to the hilltops in the distance.

Turning back to where I had entered, I saw Meher Baba still standing there. I had almost forgotten about him! Slightly embarrassed, I looked for a place to sit.

Two rocks in the circle offered and, after a moment, decided to take the larger one with the flatter surface. As I sat down, I saw Meher Baba sitting down opposite me near where we'd entered. Crossing one leg over the other, he sat swinging his foot and smiling.

He looked thoughtfully at me and nodded as if about to speak. I waited expectantly, wondering what he would say … yet he stayed silent. Maybe I should say something, and although I tried, couldn't find anything to talk about. My thoughts were still suspended, the mind absorbed in the light.

I looked back towards him and he seemed to acknowledge my attempt. Again his eyes moved, yet his lips remained still. I listened carefully, intently, straining to catch a glimpse of his voice … Perhaps I needed to change my mode of hearing, I thought.

I searched my mind for an echo of his words, trying to find the place he was coming from. Slowly, I worked my way up through layers of mind stuff and an opening appeared, like a white circle expanding out into a blue sky. Beyond the circle was a space where the light was clear, weightless and free. Moving through the opening, I became absorbed in the light, my body dissolving, my awareness merging with its awareness.

Within that light, a shining cloud swept towards me, greeting me as it neared. It was Meher Baba. A link was established, a flow of communication that was warm, loving, and intimate. Perhaps a seed of doubt arose at the veracity of this contact, for a gentle acknowledgement was received.

Then I felt myself sliding out of the light. I willed myself to stay there, but the amount of energy required was too great. Teetering on the edge, I withdrew, allowing myself to fall gently back down through layers, to find myself sitting on the rock again, enveloped in that marvelous light within the circle. Meher Baba was there, watching me, a gentle smile on his lips.

His eyes flickered again. "Do you want to continue the conversation?" he asked silently. I looked inwards for something to say but felt drained, unable to find the energy to form thoughts. Yet there no pressure from him. So, I sat peacefully on the rock, gazing out from the hilltop and enjoying his companionship, while the golden afternoon sunlight streamed through the trees, blending with the fine white light within the circle.

Streaks of Lightning
Saturday Morning

Next morning, I was driving along a broad new road that gently undulated through massive pine forests. At each rise, I could see little hills crowned with native trees, each hill appearing as an island in this sweeping ocean of pine. The sun was a warm yellow, beaming down out of a vast blue winter's sky, and I cruised along following an energy line that seemed to run under the wheels of the car. I was hoping to find a lookout, somewhere to view the many old volcano cores littered on the floor of this coastal plain.

Part Two

A sign appeared and I turned off the highway before I could read it, for a thrill of expectancy had run through me that this is what I'd been seeking. I followed the winding road as it climbed up the steep hillside, looking for any offshoots that might lead to a quiet place to meditate in the bush.

No side roads appeared and soon I was driving into a small parking area, half-filled with cars. Through the trees, I could see a café sitting at the top of the hill. People were walking about and the sound of their voices echoed across the hillside. Seeking silence and solitude for meditation, I left the café behind and headed into the forest.

As soon as I stepped out of the car park and into the trees, the energy appeared, warm and flowing. Standing for a moment, happily absorbing the vibrant essence of the bush, I looked around the tree-covered hillside. A cool fresh breeze weaved through the tall shady trees, tinged with the scent of ocean. Far below, green plains covered the lower lands. An animal trail opened in front of me and gladly I followed its narrow winding path down the hill and away from the café.

A short way along, a flat reddish rock beside the path presented itself – a likely place to sit in meditation. I looked down at the large rock and then along the path. The energy was strong but I wasn't ready to sit still yet. Deciding to come back later, I ambled along the clay trail, peering contentedly around at the new landscape.

A gap in the trees appeared and I stopped to gaze south from my vantage point, high on the hillside, to see two volcanic cores directly in front of me. They looked superb, these twin pillars of ancient earth, rising up so unexpectedly from the lush verdant plains. The nearest volcano was across a narrow valley from me, a smooth triangular-shaped mountain with dark green trees adorning its sides. Its taller companion stood just behind it, a rugged angular shaft of black rock that projected sharply up from the floor of the plain.

As I stood admiring these two volcanic mountains, I noticed a flat leaf-covered rock sitting in the shadows under the trees, just below me off the track. It looked enchanting with the dappled sunlight falling upon it; a beautiful and secluded spot to sit for meditation, I thought, and hoped the rock gave a clear view of the volcanoes.

I searched for a gap in the undergrowth that lined the track. Unable to see one, I moved further down the animal trail, eyeing the rock – but still no gap appeared. Turning around, I walked back up towards the car park, slowly examining every inch of the path for an opening, yet still couldn't find a way through the undergrowth!

Puzzled, I stopped and peered over to where the rock lay on the hillside, a short distance away through the trees. Once through the undergrowth, the slope was reasonably open and not too steep. It looked like an easy walk. Why couldn't I get to it?

Deciding to start again, I calmly moved back down to the original spot on the track where I had first seen the mountains. Gazing at the tranquil picture of the two silent volcano cores standing upon the emerald-green plains, I relaxed into the flow and turned to face the flat rock below. Allowing myself to move towards it, I stepped forward, only to be blocked by the thick bushes in front of me. Restlessly, I examined these bushes, but saw no way through their matted branches. I turned first one way and then the other, looking back along the trail where I'd already been. Frustration grew. I wanted to do my morning meditation before I went driving again!

Unable to think of another option, I decided to force a way through the undergrowth. Awkwardly, I wriggled an arm and foot into the prickly bushes, trying to create a hole, but the branches were too tough to push aside. Beginning to grow irritated, and not yet ready to give it up, I took a breath and lunged into the bushes, trying to barge a way through. Pain shot through my hand. Quickly stepping back, I saw an angry red scratch on the back of my hand. With the pain throbbing up my arm, I looked longingly down at the flat rock, but decided to take the hint, allowing this to be and accepting that it wasn't the time. Still, the rock had seemed an ideal place to meditate …

For a moment I stood undecided, wondering what to do next. I was waiting for something to happen, for the energy to reveal the purpose of this visit. Seeing no point in returning to the car, I continued on down the hill, following the animal trail through the trees.

The track petered out. I had reached a cul-de-sac. Thick bushes surrounded me. The only way to go was back. Perplexed, I slowly started back up the path towards the car park, trying to remember a time when the energy had been so strong, as palpable as the sunshine that was now beating down upon me, when something hadn't happened. Was I missing something here? I felt like I was trying to untie a knot while blindfolded, and once the clue was revealed, the knot would fall apart in my hands. But right now, I was bereft of ideas.

Yet the fears soon faded. The day was bright and warm, the energy was still high and, I reminded myself, something had *always* happened at these times.

Casting negative thoughts aside, I wandered back up the trail and was soon gazing again at the splendid picture of the two enigmatic volcanoes through the gap in the trees. But they didn't hold my attention for long.

I was turning towards the car park, allaying thoughts of returning empty-handed of experience, when I saw the flat reddish rock a short way along the trail. With a sense of relief, I walked up, settled myself expectantly upon it, and closed my eyes in meditation.

The rock was comfortable, but the meditation didn't deepen. The energy kept opening my eyes and making me want to get up and move about. It obviously wasn't a time to meditate. With the sun shining hotly down into this little protected area on the hillside, I stood up and looked around. The pathways were all closed. I had been drawn here, yet nothing had happened. Puzzled, and slightly disappointed, I started towards the car, thinking of my next destination.

On impulse, I decided to have one last look at the two volcano cores. Gazing at them through the gap in the trees, I sketched their features on to my memory, and then softly sang a note of farewell, finishing with a gentle clap of my hands. All was still. Even the voices drifting down from the café seemed muted. Standing with palms open, I imagined the sound floating softly through the air, and spreading out over the lands.

White lines of energy appeared below me, snaking their way down the hillside. Wonderingly, I stared after them as they sped through the ground like jagged streaks of lightning, and then slipped out of sight over the edge of the hill. I stood motionless, waiting ...

I turned to leave when a glowing white line appeared in the bottom of the valley between the hill on which I was standing and the nearest volcano. It raced along the narrow cleft and then shot out of the end of the valley, racing up across the open plains.

As the broad glowing line sped its way across the flatlands, other smaller lines began shooting off from its body. These fine white lines zigzagged their way out across the plain, splitting into finer lines, intersecting and connecting with each other, weaving a web upon the land. The idea arose that these flowing white lines were running through *cracks in the ground*, the lowest areas on the plain's floor. Earthquake lines, I wondered?

I kept expecting these white lines to fade, yet they remained clear and I was able to follow them with my inner sight as they disappeared beyond the horizon.

I turned back to the valley below my feet. The energy line had grown thicker and brighter, billowing out like a white mist, until it had filled the bottom of the 'V' in this little valley.

It was then that I became aware of presences under the ground. Several groups of people, a community of beings, lived within the earth here at the foot of the volcano. Drawn down within the energy, I heard a conversation taking place. A tall, thin being was speaking urgently of the need to leave, without delay. A smaller-type person replied, apparently on behalf of his race/ tribe, that a move might be required – later – but wasn't necessary now. The conversation continued, with the thin spokesperson strongly reiterating his argument, and the shorter spokesperson holding stubbornly to his own view.

I sensed there were other beings here as well. Four races who lived together. Listening intently, I leaned into the energy. Another group spoke. This group was somehow different from the others. They, too, were thin, not as tall as the first group, and dressed in silver shining clothes – or perhaps it was their aura I was picking up.

This silver group didn't appear to have originated on the planet and gave the impression of being stranded visitors, or reluctant guests. They put forward their opinion, not as strongly as the others, that they too wanted to leave, but for reasons I was unable to discern. It was difficult to fathom their minds – perhaps because they were so different. The last group did not speak. Nor did they appear to want to. Short and stocky, they kept their own counsel, yet seemed willing to go along with group consent.

I should have been surprised, amazed, bemused at witnessing such a debate. Yet I could mentally watch myself thinking these thoughts, aware of them, but not affected by them.

As I drove away from the lookout and headed east towards the coast, I thought back over the vision, and wondered at the reasons for these beings wanting to leave … and why I was to become aware of their conversation. Although I had picked up the tenor of the conversation, it hadn't appeared in word form and the notion arose that this debate had been continuing for some time. Perhaps I was picking up the residual energetic impressions from prior conversations, and these were being transferred to me – via the flowing white lines?

Interlude

I turned off the highway; the road seemed unfamiliar, wide and well-paved, cutting a swathe through a forest. This didn't look like the way to the coastal town I wanted to visit next. I was sure there was further to go, yet there was the sign pointing in its direction.

After a few moments along this strange new road, I realized I'd taken a detour. I looked for somewhere to turn around but there were few intersections on this new stretch of highway. I settled in for the short drive. The sign had said it wasn't far. But I began to grow impatient, and the few kilometers seemed to take ages to pass. With the impatience rising, I finally arrived at a little community with new houses, snuggled up against a forest. I had misread the sign indeed. The names of the two places were almost identical.

Perhaps I am meant to stop here, I thought, as I slowly drove down the short main street. But the shops didn't attract me and I saw no park to rest at. Neither was I hungry or uncomfortable. I turned around, eager to get back to the highway. My impatience abated slightly on the drive back, but I still felt pressed for time.

The turnoff to the highway soon appeared. It had only taken a few minutes to get back, yet the drive to the town had seemed so long. A quick check of the clock showed that very little time had passed. I sped along the highway, hurrying to make up the lost time, but the traffic thickened, hindering me. Relaxing, I found myself back in the flow, surprised by the detour, and wondering what it meant.

The Black Realm
Saturday Afternoon

Comfortably nestled amongst the sand dunes, I gazed out over a placid, blue ocean. Waves rolled languidly up onto the sands and sunlight glistened off their gently foaming tops. There were few people about in the cool weather. Singles and couples strolled or jogged past. I watched a man playing with his dog in the shallows, the dog leaping through the water and barking happily as he chased the waves up the beach. Although a fresh ocean breeze blew over the dunes, the warmth of the sun clung to the sands around me, bringing sweat to my brow. I closed my eyes in meditation.

Part Two

A yellow light appeared, bright behind my closed eyes. I looked up into it, feeling its soothing radiance. As its radiance increased, I wondered if it was the sun. Cautiously, I half-opened my eyes to the brilliance of ocean and sky. The sun was behind me.

Closing my eyes again, I was pleased – and relieved – to see the light still there. Gazing intently at it, I saw the yellow light transform into a star of dazzling white, its rays streaming down onto me. A longing arose to join with the light, an eagerness to ride the rays back to its source.

There came a moment of transition, a slight displacement. I was still sitting on the sand, yet I was aware of another realm as well. But when I turned my attention towards this other realm, there was only darkness. Puzzled, I opened my eyes to the sun-drenched beach. A black shadow seemed to be overlaying the sunlight, flickering on the edge of my vision. Unsure what this meant, I turned back to the meditation when I suddenly realized – I was in the Death Tunnel!

Twice before, I had accompanied friends who were passing over. With one friend, we'd stepped into a circle of light together, emerging out into a star-filled universe. With the other, we'd flown up through a long dark tunnel to the light. Eagerly, I gazed up to the star blazing high above. Who was I to accompany through the tunnel this time? No-one appeared. The light grew no closer; neither was I drawn up to it. I waited.

Perhaps, I am to travel the tunnel alone? This brought joy and hope. But am I to die? I considered this thoughtfully. The answer was unclear ... Perhaps I was simply to travel the tunnel as before – for a purpose later to be revealed.

As I focused on the light streaming down through the darkness, feelings hidden deep inside began to slowly rise. They formed a restless, seething mass in my stomach. Holding onto my meditation, I let these restless feelings slowly bubble to the surface. Watching them flow through, and out, I lightly touched these floating bubbles as they passed across my inner vision, curious to see what they were. Ideas and images arose – of death and dying.

I saw the suppressed feelings of having to, at some time in the future, deal with the transition of my parents. And other associations arose with it as well. How would the rest of the family come to terms with it? How would I cope? How would I be involved?

I thought of my wife and the same scenario arose, of the transition, how the rest of the family would deal with it, and my involvement in it. These ideas flowed outwards to encompass my children, friends, and loved ones. How would I cope? How would the others deal with it? What would my involvement be?

Slowly my thoughts turned inward towards a perspective on my own death. How would I feel to find myself at the bottom of the Tunnel, knowing I was entering the final transition? The response that arose was one of joy, bliss and freedom.

I left the beach feeling slightly disconnected from my body, stumbling on the sands as I walked back to the car. I felt I was floating just above the ground, as if gravity wasn't having its usual effect, and I was having trouble placing my feet. It was with a mental shake that I got back into the car. Being disconnected was not the way I wanted to drive through the busy coastal traffic! Settling myself, I concentrated on the drive ahead.

As I followed the main road beside the ocean, words began to scroll across my mind. They repeated themselves until I *had* to write them down. I pulled up on the side of the road and hastily made notes. A short distance along, I again left the stream of traffic to write more quickly scribbled words. It took several stops before the words completed themselves, and the message arrived. I skimmed over the notes and saw a eulogy – my own – an expression of gratitude to friends and family.

Was I going to die? I examined these feelings that were intuitively arising and could discover no trace of dying, of my death approaching, and I wondered what the lesson was …

Thinking back over my travels during the last twenty-four hours, I saw there were stories to be written. And in writing the stories a lot of information tucked away out of conscious reach would come to the fore – past experiences, insights, and more questions …

I reflected on the visit to the Meher Baba center, sitting with him on the hilltop and immersed in the fine white light within the rock circle. I thought of the strange conversation between the different races at the foot of the volcano, and how I'd stood at the bottom of the Death Tunnel. Going over these memories, a sense of contentment and peacefulness washed over me and I gave myself up to the drive.

The late afternoon winter's sun was taking on a golden glow as I turned off the highway and took the back way home, cruising along country roads and revisiting old haunts – remembering, releasing, enjoying.

The quiet road led me past an old familiar volcano; its smooth, cone-shaped sides were steeped in tall trees. Across the open fields was its larger, pyramid-shaped brother, rising up in the distance. I paused at a tiny township, the center of this locale, to wander through the few and varied shops there. Following the road again, I passed the last of the trio of old volcanoes – stunted trees dotting the top of its rocky, rounded form – until turning down a winding dirt road back into town.

The last golden rays of sunshine were streaming low through the trees when I pulled into home – to find the family arriving as well. It was impeccable timing, for we had both left from the same distant destination at different times, finding our way home along different routes, to arrive within moments of each other. It was a happy reunion and a perfect ending to the experiences of the last two days.

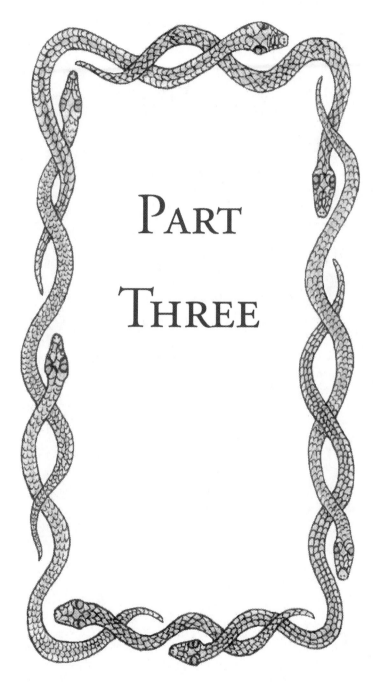

PART

THREE

CONTENTS

PART THREE

Chapter One

The Pink Room

Not long after 11 September 2001, I was concerned about a friend. We'd been chatting on-line and he'd been doing a lot of work – what he called *damage control* – and seemed tired. The thought arose to lend him/send him energy. So, with that intention in mind, I drove out to the land a day or two later.

Turning off the dusty road, I dropped down onto the creek flats and parked under the trees near the creek. I switched off the engine, and then the radio, and sat in the car listening to the sudden silence.

The land lay dreaming before me. A warm spring sun shone down on to the fields; a faint breeze sighed over the grasses. Behind the distant buzz of the cicadas was the hum of the land.

After the forty-minute drive, much of it on narrow, winding, dirt road, it was good to get out of the car and stretch. Breathing in the sweet air, I looked across the creek flats and saw that the land was drying out. The tall grasses had lost their greenish tinge and were fading from a mild brown into a bleached white. After the heat-waves of last summer, winter had brought little rain and now a new summer was almost upon us.

Having greeted the land, I ambled down to the creek. It was unexpectedly cool in the shadows of the trees, the dry leaves crunching noisily underfoot. I sat down near the circle of rocks. Clumps of green reeds stood scattered along both sides of the bank, giving a pleasant picture of abundance, but the creek had stopped flowing and only a large pool in front of the campsite remained, though it was still clear.

It's a pretty spot and I often sit there enjoying the tranquility. Today I was intending to do a meditation, but the energy wasn't conducive. As often seems to happen, what I intend to do before I arrive and what I actually end up doing are two different things (or perhaps – done at different times). So, I gathered myself and prepared to go walking.

Changing into long pants, a long-sleeved shirt, hat, gloves, and finally donning sunglasses, (experience had me taught me to be well covered lest I got scratched by the lantana) I walked from the car down to the creek again. An energetic pathway appeared before me and I followed it step-by-step, over the rocks in the creek and along the far bank. It was a pleasant walk, wandering along first one side of the creek and then the other, until I had arrived at the trees at the base of the hill. The energy there was vibrant and soothing.

I settled myself cross-legged on the ground. Barely a ripple of breeze moved the leaves on the trees, and the late winter sun was falling like a soft yellow blanket upon the earth.

Dropping into meditation, I suddenly rocked forward. How odd to twitch like that, I thought, opening my eyes. Letting my gaze roam over the soft colors and shadows of the trees and shrubs, I focused on the breath, slowing the heart rate.

I was falling back into meditation when, again, I twitched. But more than a twitch, it was a large movement that came from the waist, as if someone had put a hand on my left shoulder blade and pushed me forward. Surprised, I looked around. All was quiet. The bush was still. Even the birds seemed hushed.

I quickly spun round to see if someone was behind me, half-afraid that there might be. There wasn't, but I could still feel the imprint of a hand on my shoulder. Taking a deep breath, I wondered what was going on. Obviously something was, but what might it be?

I sat tentatively, waiting for something else to unfold but after a while, when nothing else occurred, relaxation deepened and thoughts drifted away.

For the third time I rocked forward, not quite as hard this time, but the sensation of a hand upon my shoulder was unmistakable. With my curiosity piqued, and my concentration now broken, I wondered why this was happening. And who might be doing it. Well, this obviously wasn't a time for meditation! Then I remembered that it was here, at the spot I was now sitting, that the presence had first made itself known.

Contentment arose as I sat on the connection site. Sending thoughts of him into the surrounding area, I remembered the time – the feelings, the sensations, his vibration – when I felt his presence through the ground. It was strong, confident and encouraging. I considered how close he was, but realized I wouldn't be seeing him today. As I sat there peacefully in the warm sunshine, thinking about him, my thoughts began to drift deeper toward the inner world.

A blackness arose in my mind. Then the ground dropped away and I was hurtling downwards into the earth, free falling in a place with no time or space.

The blackness gave way to the soft darkness of a tunnel and I saw my friend, the one I'd come here to help today, leading me on this underground journey. We fled downward into the earth with a sense of great haste.

A shaft of light pierced the darkness of the tunnel. Light was spilling through a cavern door. I could faintly see luminous green carvings on its sides. Quickly passing beneath the rock archway, I followed my guide inside and there, sitting by a wall, was the Inner Earth Warrior! I was surprised and pleased to see him, but even more surprised when he didn't look up or even acknowledge our presence! And then we were hurrying down an aisle and there wasn't time to consider it further.

The room seemed to be laid out in lines of empty tables or benches, and I had to keep an eye on my guide as he ducked from one aisle to another, weaving an unknown course to the far door. I looked quickly around. Everything was drab. The first time I'd visited this room, lustrous colors had radiated from the piles of weapons and treasures on the floor, streaming from the walls and dazzling the eye. Now it appeared dull, lifeless and bare. We hurried on down the aisles of the cavern.

Glancing up, I saw we were about to pass the Inner Earth Warrior. I turned to greet him, yet he gave no sign of recognition – he just sat there, mute and still. I was perplexed and a little hurt by this. After our previous contact, I thought we had gained an understanding, a sense of communion and friendship.

We were now reaching the end of the cavern, and my guide was about to disappear through a darkened doorway – with me close behind. I turned to get one last look at the warrior. He still sat motionless against the wall, head bowed, and either my vision hadn't adjusted or the room was colorless after all, for all I saw was a bland, stone-white color to everything.

We journeyed on in the dark.

Beginning to wonder when we would reach our destination, a brilliant light appeared, so unexpected and intense that I instantly shut my eyes against it. After a pause, I cautiously opened my eyes … and snapped them closed again. The light was so bright that it took a moment for the radiance to pass from my mind. Not knowing what else to do, I was standing quietly, when I realized that the light beating against my eyelids was pink! I tried blinking rapidly to get accustomed to the pink light, to look around and see where I was, but each time I opened my eyes, even a fraction, the light would sear into my brain. It wasn't painful, just of a blinding intensity.

Time passed. No-one came. Nothing happened. I could no longer sense NTA beside me. After the furious flight through the darkened underworld, to be suddenly alone, unmoving – and blinded – was so strange. How long would I have to wait for the pink light to fade?

Finally, I was able to peer through slitted eyelids and sensed, rather than saw, that I was in a room. The light shone from all directions, flooding through the walls, floor and roof, and varied from a pinkish-white to a dark red, yet the overall impression was one of a rosy hue.

I looked up to see a fiery ball of light blazing down through the ceiling. I stared at it for a moment. Was this the sun, I wondered, or another external power source? Was the light already pink before it reached the ceiling, or did the ceiling modify it?

Turning away from the blazing ball, I noticed that the ceiling seemed to have lines at different angles running through it – as if many shapes had been joined together to create it. Yet it was difficult to make out the shapes in the strong light, or gauge how big the room was.

For a moment, I became unsettled when I saw there weren't any openings in the room. I couldn't see a door or window anywhere and, consequently, no way to leave. But I relaxed when I realized that I had been *put* here and, like the other experiences, had never been *stuck,* and so would leave when the time was ripe.

The room seemed oddly familiar. As I stood bathing in the pink light, I remembered a story from Atlantean days when rooms were constructed from rose quartz, and people would enter it for healing purposes. Was this such a room?

Another indeterminable period of time passed. As I waited patiently, the pink light began to creep in through my barely-opened eyes. It slowly and gently flooded my mind, throwing light on hidden corners. A quiet exhilaration filled me. The light began to flow down into my body, and move blissfully out into my arms and legs. I became filled with its radiance, until the borders of my body were indistinguishable from the light in the room.

Awareness of body returned. Time moved on. How long was I to be here? When would the journey continue? Was there something I was supposed to be doing? I began to grow impatient, wondering what would happen next, but the light wasn't finished with me yet, it appeared. There was nothing to do but relax. It seemed a long time I waited in the pink room.

The vision changed. I was at the bottom of a tunnel. Smooth black walls encircled me, rising up to close over far above where a single point of light pierced the darkness. I was at the bottom of the Death Experience Tunnel!

Excitement arose to be in the presence of the Light again. I thought of the one I'd recently traveled with through the tunnel, and expected him to meet me. Although I sensed his presence, I remained alone at the bottom. I waited, wondering when someone would join me for the flight to the top.

No-one appeared. I peered up to the tiny point of light, shining in the blackness far above me. I willed myself to move towards it, expecting a sense of movement, of flight, but I was left motionless at the bottom of the tunnel. This was disconcerting. Before, there'd been a natural flowing to the top, an ease of movement. But now I was stuck at the bottom by myself. I looked around trying to find a clue, a hint, as to why I was here.

The walls around me were matt black – neither absorbing nor reflecting the light. There weren't any symbols, images or faces to be seen on the walls either. This, too, was unusual, for last time I'd noticed many things attached to the walls.

It seemed once again I was waiting.

Different thoughts ran through my mind as I stood unmoving in the darkness. Was I dying, I wondered? Or was this the forerunner of a future event?

A question appeared, unbidden.

Did I want to move to the Light?

Yes! Eagerness and expectancy rose within me.

Did I want to leave the physical body behind?

I pondered this …

When I had traveled the Death Experience Tunnel before, it had happened spontaneously, drawn to join a friend who was making his final transition. At that time, having attained, or been to the Light, there had been no thought of staying. It had just been a natural flow back to my normal surroundings.

Now, standing at the bottom of the tunnel and gazing up to where the Light was, it seemed to matter little whether I stayed in body or not. Both options left me feeling joyous and free.

Yet there also rose a feeling of discontentedness, of incompleteness. Were there things I wanted to finish on the earth plane? With difficulty, I tried to remember my life on earth. I could vaguely discern relationships and projects that slipped from my mind as I tried to grasp them.

Were they important? Perhaps, I thought, but only in the extinguishing of those desires. Yet I also felt I'd waited lifetimes to be able to do these things now – if only for the opportunity, and technology, that exists today.

I felt torn, in conflict. I wanted to reach up and join with the Light, yet stay in body. I wanted to explore the universe, free of cumbersome physicality, but realized a physical body was needed to finish the projects already started. Was this ego? I didn't know. I longed for the Light, yet somehow feared the consequences of attaining it.

Chapter Two

Initiation under the Rock

The Final Resistance

Lying down on the floor of the lounge room, I closed my eyes, filling my mind with an image of Uluru, silhouetted against an early evening sky. Almost immediately my body began drifting away, and a light began to fill the darkness behind my eyelids. The light quickly increased, pouring down upon me until, with a rush, it crashed into my mind.

I sat up, drowsily. I must have fallen asleep. The white light was still vivid in my mind. As I sat there, it slowly drained away, retreating and contracting to a spot in the center of my forehead.

The clock said 1.00 am. Roughly two hours had passed. Groggily, I got up and headed for the bedroom. I should write some notes, I thought, before I fall asleep, for I knew that much of the dream would be forgotten by morning. But I was tired, and my only wish was to climb into my comfortable bed.

I lay down and snuggled under the blankets. With a sigh, I contentedly leaned my head back onto the pillow, feeling it sink blissfully down after lying on the hard floor. With my eyes closed, the white light began to glow brightly in my mind again and I remembered the vivid image of running through the desert under a midnight sky. I thought of the diary on the bedside table tugging at my attention, but I ignored it.

The little one moaned loudly in her sleep, pulling me awake. I lay quietly, listening. She began to cry, the sound muffled by her blankets. I rolled out and stumbled into her room, groping my way in the dark. I reached out to find her bed and cracked my shin hard on the metal frame. Did it hurt! I hopped around swearing softly in the dark, as flashes of pain echoed through my assaulted shinbone. I was wide awake now, so as soon as the little one was settled, I took the hint and scribbled out notes in the diary. Sleep came peacefully after that.

Next morning, I re-read the notes. Already I could feel memories slipping away, yet I also knew that as I transferred the notes onto the computer and expanded on them, other details would arise and things buried would surface.

I stood inside the cavern. In front of me burned a campfire, its orange flames casting flickering shadows onto the rough walls and domed rock ceiling. Two others stood beside me, their black bodies shining in the firelight and their eyes gleaming in anticipation as they turned to me in welcome and acknowledgement. On the other side of the fire stood Knowledge.

We waited with respect and quiet excitement. Standing over the fire, we each in turn poured water gently onto it, offering up the steam as a token of our Gratitude (to Spirit) and esteem (of the elder).

He leaned forward and, taking the wooden bowl, held it high above his head. Slowly he lowered it, peering into it as if reading the small pool of water that was left in the bottom. He paused, holding the bowl out in front and looked sternly up at us, holding our eyes one by one. Fiercely did he glare at us, but it could not dampen our enthusiasm, for it shone in our eyes.

Then he moved forward, took our hands to form a circle, and began to sing, to croon, almost to moan. The soft, slightly sad, singing gently reverberated around the cave. Our attention was caught up as we listened, drawn by the intensity of his voice. He paused, the chant fading into whispers amongst the shadows of the rocks, and then he began to sing again, catching the lingering echoes and building upon the sound.

The resonance increased after each pause. We were lifted upon the soft wings of his dirge-like chant as the waves of sound rolled out further and further.

The chanting grew louder as he called upon the ancestors to witness; the soft sighing of the cavern walls murmured in response. He hailed the Great Mother and we were reminded to care for Her, for the earth sustained us. Finally he called down the Sky Spirits, and shining beings arrived to smilingly greet us. And then we were flung from the cave, riding on a thread of light, propelled outwards by the elder's song.

Through the light we flew, the shining threads of my companions diverging from my own flight path. Realm after realm swept by. Forests, cities and arenas of light flashed past in myriad haste, as this undulating thread of light bisected the dimensions. I was carried along its exhilarating journey, sitting atop this thread that twisted and turned, stretching out before me and disappearing into the endless dimensions.

The song changed. Instantly my attention was caught. I turned in my seat, listening, alert. He called again, his voice ringing through the dimensions. There was a pressure in his voice, an insistence that irresistibly hailed me. Still I was swept along by this silver thread, yet now distracted from the vistas that fled past. For there arose a deep longing, a need to understand the meaning in this new song. I tried to turn the thread of light, to search for the elder's voice, but its flight continued unabated, flinging me with relentless haste through the dimensions.

Hesitantly, desperately, I reached down to gently ask this silver thread I rode upon, to plead with it ... and at the slightest touch, it obeyed.

We came to a halt in a large courtyard surrounded by adobe buildings, startling a well-dressed man and lady dining in bright sunshine. A servant carrying a tray down the steps towards them stopped and looked up at me open-mouthed. And then I was gone, the thread instantly following my thoughts.

I searched, riding the currents, weaving a path through innumerable realms, listening to his continuous chant that urged us to follow the song, and find our own pathway back to its source. I flew this way and that, to stop and listen to the chant, and then onwards again, to stop and listen.

I grew closer ... and lost it. I desperately searched again and caught a glimpse of him! And then he was gone. With renewed hope, I slowed, peering into the dimensions, turning in tighter and tighter circles, to finally arrive at a quiet place in the light. There, hiding behind an astral palm tree, was the old man sitting cross-legged, and smiling.

In the cave, the Song changed. He began to dance. We were moved to join with him in this strange dance, our hands clasped together in the circle, our eyes turned upwards. The energy began to build. The circle spun faster and faster. I was being drawn up into a vortex ...

Then he sang the shapes of the Universe. And we were spread-eagled, upright in the Light, reverberating ecstatically to the sounds. Echo after echo rang through my companions and I.

We were picked up and tossed like leaves in a great wind, and fell on a gentle breeze. We were lost in a spiral storm, and flung to the far reaches of the universe. We were sent home and came back of our own free will – gladly, willingly.

We became One, then Nothing, then Everything. We were No-one and Everyone. Open or closed, our eyes saw everything.

It was dark. I was lying outside, surrounded by sand, staring up at a low thin moon in the night sky. The stars twinkled serenely down over the desert; a hint of morning scented the air. The great monolith was faintly outlined on the horizon. Beside me lay another, younger, slender, transfixed as I was with the sky above.

Rising out of the sand, I saw a campfire flickering in the blackness and walked towards it. Someone was there waiting for us. He was older, with a look full of mixed emotion – sad, it seemed, as he sat staring into the flames of the fire, yet stern when he turned towards my approach. The younger joined me, and together we stood outside the circle, while the older sat on one of the large flat rocks around the campfire and gazed back at us.

I began to dance. A dance of inner joy. Joining with the fire, I moved in harmony with the flames as they flared higher and higher into the night sky ...

And then I was running. Through the darkened desert I sped, weaving a path through the small shrubby trees and undergrowth, the soft sand slippery underfoot. The mind was calm, yet the body moved swiftly. I glanced to my left and behind. The younger – the one who had agreed to meet me here – was following. Together we ran through the desert.

A shadow appeared. I veered around it and then sprinted forward again. The logical mind clicked in. How did I know it was there? It was almost totally dark; there were only vague glimpses of the horizon and at my feet nothing could be seen, yet I had distinctly seen something on the ground – a solidified shadow to be avoided. I wondered about this as the body ran effortlessly on, weaving a path first one way and then the other, the younger following faultlessly. Then I gave myself up to it. Together we ran calmly, steadily, and swiftly, through the night.

The pathway became a tunnel. Down through the earth I swept, following the winding tunnel alone until, there, waiting for me, was the Inner Earth Warrior.

He turned and led me onwards through the tunnel until we arrived at a cavern, a cavern I did not recognize, and which he proudly showed me.

I turned to him and said, half-aggrieved and half-pleased, "You're my friend!"

Looking at me calmly, he said with slight surprise, "Of course."

At our first meeting he had challenged and pressured me. The next time, even though I thought we'd reached an understanding, he'd totally ignored me. So, I was totally taken by surprise at the warmth and pride he displayed when showing me his home today.

He brought me to the birthing pools. The colors of the creek were suddenly vivid after the darkness of the tunnel, and my eyes drank in the glowing astral greens of the trees, palms and ferns covering the banks. The multi-colored rocks scattered on the creek's bed shone with an inner life, as the clear waters calmly twisted a gentle path above them.

And there, on the creek's rocky floor, was the Dreamsnake. Leaving the Inner Earth Warrior to meet with another, I walked over to stand before this Ancient Serpent once again, its head high above me, its mouth gaping open. It was lifeless, unaware, drained of color, with only a few black patches appearing on its white exterior. It reminded me of a hollow tube or tunnel, a tool waiting to be activated, or used.

And I was back, lying on the lounge room floor, the outline of my body still dissolved in the light. As I lay there, absorbed in the radiance, a series of images passed before my mind's eye, the last notes recorded in my diary.

Imprinted on a mottled green background was the shape of a kangaroo. It faded and then the outline of a wallaby appeared, followed by the impression of a dingo, echidna, emu, winged snake and lotus flower.

Chapter Three

The Birthing Pools

Monday 18 March 2002

Standing chest deep in the cool, clear waters of the circular birthing pool, I waded over to the vertical rock wall. Leaning forward, I rested my forehead against it, and closed my eyes.

With my head still touching the wall, I opened my eyes to see a large red rock lying on the bottom near my feet. Through the wavering waters, it looked remarkably straight-edged and I automatically stepped back to pick it up. Feeling the connection break once I left the wall, I leaned back and placed my forehead against its hard surface. Opening my eyes, I again saw the large rock through the water. With a breath, I ducked down and lifted it out, surprised at how heavy it was. And how large it was! For the bottom of this little pool was usually covered in small creek pebbles washed down by the rains.

I climbed out and sat on the water-smoothed rock opposite the wall, balancing the rock in both hands. It was a long rectangular shape, nearly the length of my forearm and slightly thicker, its edges well-defined with a line of white crystal running through it. It had a luxurious feel and, like many of the rocks here in the creek, was a deep rich red color.

One face presented itself, the most regular of the long rectangular faces. This face curved slightly in. A persistent thought arose – of placing my forehead on the curved surface – a curious thought ... Going with the flow, I lifted the rock up and bent my head, touching my forehead to its wet surface.

It was warm, even the water clinging to the stone was warm, and the long rock fitted perfectly around the curve of my forehead. I held the stone away from me and, like the rock wall before, felt the connection break. Quickly I pressed my forehead back against it, holding it there with my elbows on my knees to support it, and felt comfort flow into me. Within the connection, I began to explore the rock, moving into it, and through it ...

The rock grew heavy. I lowered it, easing my aching arms, and gazed out to where the sunlight was falling brightly onto the lower pool. I ran my eyes up the two steep cliff faces at the far end of the pool, to the tall thin palm trees sitting on their tops. Above the trees on the surrounding hills floated a tranquil blue sky. Resting the wet rock in my hands, I scanned the slopes for the presence of the elders.

Several times before, rocks had come to hand while at this creek and each time there'd been an impulse to leave it hidden, tucked away for later. Wondering where to leave this rock, I looked over the creek banks. One side of the creek was a tangled weave of prickly vines and shrubs crowded between the trees, the other a sheer climb up bare rock faces. There was nothing that drew me.

Moving over to on the narrow lip where the water runs out of the circular pool and down a smooth sloping rock face to the lower pool, I considered what to do. I held the rock out before me, and asked aloud whether to take it home. The light dimmed over the tiny valley. "Shall I leave it here?" I queried. The light grew brighter. Repeating the two questions brought the same replies.

Content with letting the rock go, I decided to throw it into the pool below. As I gently swung the rock back and forth, I studied my motions and, feeling I was in the flow, released it. The rectangular rock arced through the air to land with a satisfying splash, and disappeared in to the muddy water at the base of the rock face.

I wandered back along the creek with a lingering undercurrent of regret, of something left unfinished. As I reviewed the events surrounding the releasing of the long rock, I wondered, again, about leaving such an item somewhere. Yet, I felt I had acted within the moment, and nothing distinctive had made itself known as a hiding place.

A few days later, via a series of synchronistic events, I was inspired to go back and find the rock. No rain had fallen, so the lower pool would still be shallow, if dirty. The rock wouldn't be hard to find.

Parking the car on the side road, I wandered down the narrow overgrown pathway to the creek. Just along the bank is a large smooth rock that projects out into the water. I often sit there, meditating or enjoying the harmony of nature. Today, I paused a moment, standing silently upon it. Finding no desire to linger, I continued on down the creek, past the Rainbow Rock and towards the opening in the massive rock that spans the valley walls.

Following the long shallow pool in through the cleft in the wall, I arrived at the circular pool cut deep into the rock, and jumped in without hesitation. The water was beautiful – cool and refreshing. Slowly wading over to the rock wall, I placed my forehead against it, seeking the snake tunnel. There was no response. An image of *spider* arose. I stepped back and searched the wall. There, not far from me, was a big spider clinging to the wall with a large sac on its black underbelly. Acknowledging the spider, and then asking for permission to enter, I placed my forehead against the wall again.

A faint light appeared in the darkness. I peered into it, watching. The light grew brighter and there came a sense of movement. My mind was being drawn into the light. Down, I quickly traveled through a twisting tunnel, and there appeared the Snake/Dragon, sleeping. He slowly stirred, and opened an eye.

"What are you doing here?" he asked. Looking for an honest answer, I replied, "Just for a visit." Not wanting to disturb his rest any longer, I broke the connection, yet glad to have traveled the snake tunnel again.

I splashed in the pool, lazily floating on my back in the clear soft water, gazing up at the blue sky peeping between the overhanging branches. The spider, I noticed, hadn't moved from its position on the wall.

Finally, I hauled myself out of the pool and stood on the lip, looking down the rock face into the spreading lower pool. I imagined releasing the rock again, and eyed the section of water it would have landed in. An idea from the book *Tom Sawyer* arose, of throwing a pebble into the pool and seeing where it lands before starting to search. Quickly finding a small stone, I stood on the lip, and boyishly threw it into the water, deciding against adding the incantation, as is written in the book. Feeling slightly foolish, I watched as the stone dropped with a small splash into the water, the ripples quickly disappearing as the surface of the pool smoothed over again. It landed very close to where I expected the rock to be, yet somehow I was left feeling somewhat deflated.

Carefully, I climbed down the smooth rock face with my wet feet, and stood on the bank nearest to where I thought the rock would have landed. The water was dark and dirty, the bottom hidden. I gingerly eased one foot into the pool, testing its depth, when my foot started to slide down the side of the gravel bank. Knowing it was shallow, I stepped out into the pool, surprised to see the water rise up to my thighs.

Rolling up my shorts, I waded slowly through the water. Being closer to the pool hadn't brought greater visibility. The water was so muddied I could barely see my legs, and my footsteps were disturbing the moss on the bottom, bringing it floating to the top.

It was only a few steps to the most likely place for the rock to have landed and, knowing it was rather large, expected it to be easy to find. Cautiously, I felt around with my feet on the sandy bottom, wary of sticks or branches that may be submerged. Nothing. I tentatively began searching again.

My foot bumped against something on the bottom. I felt it with my toes, but my expectation quickly evaporated when I realized it was too small for the rock I was looking for. Still, I reached through the dirty water and picked it up, disappointed and curious at the same time. It was roughly rectangular, deep red, and like the other rock, also had a vein of white crystal running through it. It didn't attract me as much as the other, but the crystal was intriguing, so, placing it on the bank, I went back to the search.

Further out in the pool, the bottom dipped down into a narrow channel. Surprised I hadn't found the rock already, I slowly inched along the sandy channel, wondering if it had somehow slipped down into it. Still nothing. I started a spiral search, wading through the water in bigger and bigger circles, until I was beyond where the rock would have landed, and had reached a shallow section in the middle of the pool. Standing in the ankle-deep water, I looked at the area I had covered, bemused. The bottom was layered in sand and gravel, and such a large rock shouldn't be hard to find. How could I have missed it? There'd been no rain – only a trickle of water was flowing down the rock face – so the bottom couldn't have changed.

Half-heartedly, I began to search again, and then decided to have a rest. Climbing up onto the bank, I sat down under a shady tree and drifted into meditation. The forest was peaceful and still. The water tinkled gently down the rock face behind me. A few birdcalls piped through the trees.

Afterwards, I slowly went over the area again, repeating the spiraled search pattern, but still the rectangular rock didn't turn up. Resigned, I picked up the new rock I'd found and scrambled back up the rock face. I was intending to continue on up the creek to the car, but the water was so inviting in the round pool that I dived in again. The spider was still clinging to the rock wall.

Placing my head against the hollow in the wall, the light opened and I quickly ran down the tunnel. The snake was coiled at the bottom. I told him that it was time for me to leave. Opening both eyes, he looked at me and said, "You [need to] go [t]here." And he showed me a mountaintop.

The outline of that mountain was well known to me, a familiar feature on the land, and several times I had considered the long climb to the plateau at its top. It would be a difficult journey scaling its steep, rocky side, yet the desire to go exploring grew within as I beheld its image in my mind.

Walking up the creek, my thoughts wandered back over the events of the day. I realized I'd placed my forehead against the rock wall three times: the first time nothing had happened, the second time the Snake had spoken, and on the third, he'd given me a vision.

I had also searched the lower pool for the rectangular rock three times. And this was the third time I'd been at the pools when a rock had come to hand and, although I'd wanted to save it for later, nothing had appeared as a likely hiding place. A feeling of surety arose with the thought of the next time a rock arrived.

Chapter Four

Be Gentle from the Heart

The heat of the day lingered in the evening air. Under the streetlight on the corner of a quiet back street was a large mango tree, its fruit littered and rotting on the ground. Beneath it stood three youths, perhaps drawn by the sounds of the Christmas party opposite.

We were carrying our musical gear out to the van when I dimly spied them standing under the mango tree, holding bottles in their hands. Bill, laden down with guitar amps beside me, cast a wary eye towards the boys who were watching us.

"Hello," I said, nodding as we walked past. Seeing this as an invitation, two of them started following us to the van and pestering us.

"Got a cigarette?" one asked.

"Got a coke?" asked the other.

We ignored them, and with determined steps lugged our equipment across the darkened street.

They stood uncomfortably close while we loaded the back of the van, still asking for smokes or cokes. "Can't do that," I said repeatedly. "Won't do that!" in the end.

I climbed into the back while Bill took the driver's seat, and we waited in the dark for the last member to arrive, the two boys lingering beside my window. The third boy still stood under the mango tree, his profile silhouetted by the streetlight. Running out of patience and muttering to himself, Bill went back inside to get Missy, leaving me alone with the two youths standing silently nearby.

As soon as Bill had disappeared into the night, one of the boys, a short thin youth, left his position outside my window and began to walk quickly around the front of the van.

I watched him intently from the back seat, and then, suspicious of his ambitions, rushed to lock the two front doors. I reached down to undo the seatbelt and lunged forward, only to be thrown back into my seat. The seatbelt hadn't released. I fumbled with the catch and then lunged forward again – only to be thrown back once more. I was stuck in a strange seatbelt in the dark! The youth reached the driver's door and lifted the handle. Panic started to rise.

I deliberately calmed myself with a deep breath, envisaging peace, and gently reached down toward the buckle, allowing the subconscious to find the catch and … still it wouldn't release! The thin boy had now opened the door and was peering into the darkened cabin. Panicking, I hammered madly at the catch.

Then I was gliding forward to stand between the two front seats. The boy stood unmoving beside me, half-leaning into the car. Was he drunk, I wondered? I scanned the dashboard and the seats in the semi-dark, lit only by the distant streetlight on the corner. What was he after?

The keys! Where were they? Had Bill left them behind? It was too dark to see if they were still in the ignition. I reached over and waved my hand underneath the steering wheel. There was a jangling sound and I grabbed at them, the youth watching closely at the door. They wouldn't come out. I fumbled and jerked at them wildly, and then the keys were in my hand, and in the next instant, I was sitting in the back seat.

The youth turned to me, his eyes glaring.

"Why you do that?" he demanded.

Silence.

"Why you do that?" he repeated angrily.

"This not your car," I said from the back seat, trying to sound indignant.

"This your car?" quietly asked the other youth, a big, solid lad, standing outside my window.

Startled by the unexpected voice beside me, I turned to him. "This MY car," I replied – firmly and friendly. Smiled.

(Why was I talking in some kind of pigeon English? I had never spoken like this before – talking to them like small children rather than as young men.)

The thin boy stood glaring at me for a moment and then stepped back uncertainly from the car door, leaving it open, and began walking around the van to where the other youth stood. I quickly leaned over the seats, pulling the driver's door shut and locking both the front doors.

The two stood a short distance away from my open window – the large lad and the thin youth – not moving or talking, their faces cast in deep shadow from the streetlight behind. Warily I watched them, waiting for any more untoward movements. The large lad hadn't moved throughout this little drama and now I cautiously studied him. There was something gentle about him, something appealing …

The back street was deserted. There was no sign of the other two returning. I glanced over at the third youth still standing under the mango tree. His outline was tense, his body slightly hunched over, the bottle in his hand. I noticed that not one of the boys had taken a drink from their bottles yet.

An impetus to speak arose. I could feel it in my abdomen, rising up into my chest, but quickly suppressed it, not wanting to antagonize these boys with an untimely comment. Again, it forced its way upwards into my chest. I turned to examine these words before they were spoken, yet hearing only silence, struggled to restrain this inner urge.

The impetus rose irresistibly to my throat. Then I relaxed, feeling the words were safe to say, and listened attentively to what would come. But they did not come straight away, and I leaned forward in my seat, gazing intently up through the open window at the two youths, as the words struggled in my mouth.

"Be gentle," I heard myself say, tapping fingers on my chest, "from the heart."

There was a pause. Nobody moved.

Again the words were spoken. "Be gentle. From the heart," and tapped the end of my fingers on my breastbone. And then sat back in the seat. Neither of the boys moved. All was still.

As the moment stretched, I looked for something to say to break the silence. I turned to the large quiet boy, wanting to engage him in conversation, and said with a smile, "You go *walking*? You go walking in the *bush*?" and nodded my head towards the west. There was no response, so I tried another approach.

"They take you walking? *They* take you walking – out in the bush?" They were silent for a moment and then, taking my meaning, both nodded. "They show you the *places*?" I asked twice. This caught their attention and they glanced at each other.

The big lad quietly said, "Where you from?"

I told him the name of the distant town where I lived. The thin boy suddenly revealed white teeth in a big smile, and happily told me that he came from a town not far from there, surprising me with his quick change in attitude. The third boy called out his town of origin animatedly from his position under the mango tree. He, too, lived not far from my town. I hadn't realized he could hear us from over there.

This was the first time in the conversation there had been a connection. They looked at me with eyes gleaming in the dark. Then the quiet boy moved up closer, leaning on the windowsill, and softly told me that he lived here, in this town. His body posture and vibration were very gentle. I began to like him. The thin youth also moved closer, totally dropping the aggressive attitude.

"Who you?" the quiet boy asked.

I was unsure how to answer and thought for a moment. "I white fella," and then, thinking that it might be taken as an aggressive or separatist remark, I pointed to them, "You black," and then using a gesture to include all of us said, "We all the same." The last remark was said rather vehemently.

The quiet boy seemed unsure of that, but the thin youth nodded in agreement, again surprising me.

The conversation was coming to an end.

"What's your name?" I asked the big quiet boy next to me.

"Raymond," he said with surprising strength and pride in his voice. Peering in at me, he gently asked, "What's your name?"

"Rodney," I replied, and then added as an after thought, "DreamSnake – Rodney DreamSnake."

His lips moved and I wondered what he was saying. I couldn't hear anything, and then realized that he was silently repeating the name to himself. And then his eyes lit up. "Rodney DreamSnake!" He turned smilingly to the thin boy, who nodded eagerly back at him. I was baffled by their response, and still am …

We were quiet for a few moments, knowing this encounter was soon to end and knowing it had been good.

"What you got?" I asked, looking at their bottles, thinking they would say rum or another alcohol.

"Paint!" the quiet boy and thin youth said in unison. And together they lifted the clear glass bottles to their noses and took a deep sniff. Seeing what they were doing, the third youth lifted his bottle in salute, and also held it to his nose.

Bill and Missy appeared from out of the darkness, heading towards us. We still had a few moments left to ourselves. I tried to hide my surprise at their answer yet, strangely, the judgemental mind was suspended. I struggled to bring it to the fore, but it was too difficult, so I let it go. And then again, I reasoned, I'd had a few more beers than usual tonight at the break-up. Who was I to judge!

The others were nearly within hearing distance.

"Hey," I began, intending to say, "Take care," by way of farewell, but "Be good," came out instead. I was as startled by my words as they were, and they shifted uneasily. I thought desperately of something to smooth it over, wanting to leave on good terms. Instinctively, I reached over to put my hand on the quiet boy's arm where he had it resting on the windowsill.

"Take care, brother," I said gently to him, and then turned to nod and smile at the thin youth. The quiet boy stepped back, surprised when I put my hand on his arm, but seeing the others arriving, he quietly said goodbye, too. I looked over to the third boy. He hadn't moved the whole time, still standing underneath the mango tree. He lifted a hand, his silhouette one of happy acknowledgment, and I waved back.

I unlocked the front doors, Bill and Missy took their seats, and the two aboriginal boys moved respectfully back from the van. They wanted to linger, to lengthen our time together, and so did I. Our last moments together were silently shared, until final farewells were quietly exchanged as the van moved off.

There were things to talk about as we drove away, so I had to push the encounter regretfully to the back of my mind. It was only later, as we were driving out of town and settling into the twenty-minute drive back to the shed site, that I was able to wonder at the unusualness of the event.

What did it mean? I wondered, and how much would they remember of it? Where was the connection? Perhaps, later, understanding would come, but for the moment it felt good to sit quietly, feeling the energies of the encounter deep inside. And how they'd leapt at the name! What did it mean to them? Would they tell the others? What would the others think?

And then an instance earlier in the week came to mind that seemed to be connected with tonight. And I understood there was more to come. And I wondered who the *People* were …

Chapter Five

Rock of the Elders

It took a while to get out of bed the next morning; my head was still groggy from the party the night before. Eventually, I rolled out, dragged some clothes on, and stumbled up to the shed site. Bill was already there, standing on a ladder and arranging a sheet of corrugated iron over a doorway. As I stood watching him, longing for coffee and waiting for the energy to rise, a rock on the ground caught my eye. Without thinking, I started walking over to pick it up. Bill, perched on the ladder, glanced down when he saw me moving over towards him. Not wanting to distract him, I stopped and stepped back, studying the rock while I waited. I couldn't take my eyes off of it!

It was small, with smoothly rounded edges, and a reddish-purple color in the early morning sun. But I was struck by how odd the rock looked, sitting there in the open, and by my eagerness to hold it in my hand. The mind was having trouble waking up this morning, but I forced it forward and made it think.

How had this rock come to be here? Had it been accidentally dropped? Or had someone placed it there? This area was totally bare of rocks. I'd been picking up the rocks from around the shed because I'd stumbled awkwardly a few times when carrying heavy materials, and didn't want to risk an accident. So it was all the more surprising to see a rock here, all by itself, on the most walked upon piece of ground that had been packed hard by the vehicles.

Another thing that struck me as odd was how Bill was working here this morning – at the front of the shed – when we'd slowly been working our way around the back over the last few days.

I stood baffled, my eyes on the rock, considering it.

And the peculiar idea came to mind that perhaps it had been transported here. I smiled wryly to myself at the thought, but the idea took hold. I looked around, trying to sense energy. A line was running away from me, diagonally through the trees towards the highway. As I peered along the energy line, a dark cloud appeared against the trees, and through the cloud came a sense of power. Following the line further, a vague image arose of hills, but I could make no more of it. I turned back to watch Bill.

Finishing up, he stepped down off the ladder, and I casually walked over and picked up the rock. I glanced at it in my hand for a moment, this small smooth deep-red stone, and then slipped it into my pocket.

Missy appeared, and soon we were back into it, the rock bumping against my leg as I walked. I reached down and felt it through the fabric of my pants. There was a thrill of excitement in the anticipation of holding it, yet I didn't want to short-circuit the energies before I had a chance to examine them. The morning wore on.

I was becoming impatient by mid-morning and, seeing that little was happening, took a break for morning tea and found a quiet corner.

Slowly and carefully, I dipped my hand into my pocket and felt my fingers close over the rock's smooth, and surprisingly warm, surface. I felt like a naughty boy with a guilty pleasure, hiding away from prying eyes. Drawing it out, I held it to the light, having my first good look at it.

It was an unusual shape, not readily definable, taking the appearance of a flat inverted kidney bean. It wasn't large, yet had a firm weight and sat comfortably in my hand. I could almost close my fingers totally around it. But it was the color that instantly drew my attention. It was a dark reddish-brown, more red perhaps than brown, for it seemed to change in the light as I moved it around. Its color reminded me of the rocks at the birthing pools at home. And that was another odd thing about it. It had the smoothness of a creek rock. There weren't any creeks or rivers around here. The sharp-edged and shattered rocks around the shed we were building had been dug out of the side of the hill with a bulldozer to create the level area for this site.

One surface of the rock was rounded, and fitted neatly into the base of my fingers. The other side had a shallow dip in it. I ran my thumb lightly over this slight depression in the rock, stroking the smooth surface.

Yet there was a sense of anti-climax as I gazed down on this dark red rock. It didn't call or tingle in my hand. Nothing came to mind; no connection appeared.

I was rolling it around in the cup of my hand, idly pondering it – when I nearly dropped it! With a start of surprise, and a rapid increase in the heart rate, I caught it just before it rolled off the flat of my hand. I breathed a sigh of relief. I didn't think it would break, but I was trying to treat it gently!

The impetus for work returned, and regretfully I slid it back into my pocket. As the day progressed, the weight of the rock tugging on my pants was a constant reminder of its presence. I thought of the boys from the night before. Were the two events connected? I had already scribbled some notes on the meeting with the three youths, and was intending to write more in the diary tonight. Perhaps that would help connect me with the *red crystal rock*, as I had come to call it.

Chapter Six

Dance of the Elders

I spent a quiet evening, wanting time to relax and focus before bed, giving me a chance to explore this new and interesting phenomenon, the little red rock that had come to hand. After the air conditioning had cooled down the caravan, I lay on the bed with a sheet draped over me to ward off the cool air.

Why was this device here? Who had sent it? Where had this red hand rock come from? During the day, the idea had arisen that it was somehow connected with the encounter with the aboriginal boys the night before.

Was it a thank you? A progression … ?

The Shadow on the Hill

To complete this story, we need to backtrack to the first day when the three of us had arrived to erect a large shed out in the country. Having unpacked, Bill and I had gone for a drive, late in the afternoon, to get supplies. It was a ten-minute drive to a solitary outpost on the highway. It consisted of an old store, renovated, but still retaining an uneven, wooden floor – probably from the time it'd first been built – and a phone box outside I used to phone home.

On the drive there, I had noticed a series of rounded hills sitting on flat, grassed lands and, although this area was new to me, these hills looked fairly different to the surrounding landscape. Amongst the hardy trees covering the hills, I could see large patches of exposed rock, and cliff faces with huge boulders lying at their feet. The hills all seemed to be joined together, flowing into each other. There was something about them that drew me …

By the time we'd finished our jobs at the shop and had begun the drive back, the hills had slipped from my mind, but as they came into view again, this time on the passenger side of the car, I had another chance to study them.

I was following the line of hills with my eyes when I was surprised by something that'd escaped my attention the first time. Sitting below the horizon line, and protruding out from the middle of the hills, was a huge rounded outcrop of rock. This dark-brown, stone globule bulged out from near the base of the hills, its face pockmarked with holes or tiny caves.

As I gazed at this fascinating and prominent figure, a grey mist began to gather in front of it. The mist quickly grew until the rock became obscured. A power seemed to be emanating from it … And then an aboriginal face appeared, overlaid upon this swirling mist.

I watched until it was gone from view, and then sat back, enjoying the golden afternoon sunlight falling across the wide open fields as we sped down the highway. A curious and happenstance event, I thought, and wondered what it could mean.

And now forward as …

The Fire Circle

I lay on my bed in the thick darkness of the caravan, the red rock cupped in my open palm at my side. I struggled for calmness with the pent-up emotions of excitement, anticipation and curiosity whirling around inside. It took time to slow the heart and breath until, finally, I began drifting off. In between the waking and sleeping state, I found my other hand lying on a spear. I realized it was a dream spear, yet I could feel the grain of the wood and its smoothness under my fingers. It was strangely comforting to touch. I opened my eyes and peered down in the semi-darkness only to find the bed bare, yet when I lay back, there it was again, lying under my hand.

The spear tugged at my attention…

It was night. I was standing on the edge of a circle of people. Dressed only in a loincloth, the spear and rock in either hand, I faced towards a blazing fire in the center. On either side of me in the circle stood women and children. The women looked at me warmly or curiously, the children shyly or fearfully. On the right hand side of the fire were a group of elders, their decorated faces flickering in the orange flames. There were other faces also dimly discernible, standing outside the circle of light. Many were dressed in white clay and markings.

I moved forward to stand in front of the fire, clearly visible to all, letting their gazes fall upon me, and then squatted down on my haunches, waiting.

From the right stepped an Elder – tall, decorated, grey-bearded – and spoke in a clear, authoritative voice. He asked a question. I stood to answer. Words fell from my lips, flowing out in a liquid language. He asked another question. Again, I answered, the words rolling off my tongue. At some point, I realized I didn't actually understand what I was saying. I could feel and hear the words as they came out of my mouth, but they made no sense. It was disconcerting and I listened closely to the conversation, desperately trying to find the key that would unlock the language and open up understanding.

The conversation continued. The Elder asking short abrupt questions, while I answered in a steady and defined way. And then suddenly I was disconnected from the scene, standing to one side, and watching this conversation between 'myself' and the Elder. And, even more strangely, this new perception didn't interrupt the flow of events.

From this other viewpoint, I could see myself standing tall and proud in the firelight, smooth-skinned and well muscled, a warrior in his prime. I looked towards the tall Elder, unsure if he was aware of this other disconnected me.

(On the periphery of my vision was another pair of eyes. Someone else was there, standing between this warrior aspect of myself and me. I remember the eyes being at waist level. Was it another person, a child, an animal ... ?)

The door to understanding didn't open and the questions and answers continued until, with a ring in his voice, the Elder asked a final question. This question was instantly recognizable as, "By what authority do you proclaim yourself?"

All silently watched while I pondered.

At this stage, the lessons learnt suggested that such things were not spoken about openly. So I was curious why he had asked the question. Then the answer came. Holding the Elder's gaze, I sent him the message, unspoken, with the eyes.

Then, wary of ego creeping in, I sent my thoughts inwards and upwards, and silently said a Name. And everyone left. The women and children standing nearby fled, and the elders also hurried off. I was left alone – and confused – in the center of the deserted circle. Why had the internally spoken name caused such an effect?

The Dancers

As I stood there, bewildered and silent in front of the blazing fire, a Kun'diri man stepped forward into the empty circle. Dressed in a furred head covering with red cloths tied on his arms, his face and body were smeared in intricate patterns of white clay. He was a little man, his face lined with age, yet he emitted an aura of Strength, Power and Good Will. He looked towards me, and I wondered if he was also going to question me.

I squatted down in front of the fire again, waiting for him to speak.

Movement caught my eye. Glancing up, I saw to my left, at the far top of the circle, a line of white clay-clad warriors emerging from out of the darkness. And they were dancing! Surprised, I watched the line grow longer as they moved into the light of the fire. I turned towards the Kun'diri. He was gazing at me steadily. Seeing no change in his expression, I turned back to this unexpected spectacle.

The line of warriors continued from out of the darkness, slowly dancing towards the top of the circle; their hair, faces and bodies were covered in white markings that made them look ghost-like in the flickering of the fire.

My eyes were drawn to the leader of the line. I watched him dance, moving to some unheard song, his arms and legs giving expression to his inner melody.

Running my eye down the line, I realized that each warrior had his own distinct dance that somehow blended into an overall pattern, harmonious with the others. It was difficult to discern their markings, yet there was the impression that each warrior was painted in a separate and individualistic way, as personal as his dance.

Another line of warriors appeared, this time from the right, dancing out of the darkness and heading towards the top of the circle. They, too, were painted in white clay markings, and danced their separate dances in harmony. There were now two lines of painted warriors, slowly moving towards each other across the fire from me. I didn't know which line to watch! I glanced over to the Kun'diri, but his face was turned towards the lines of dancing warriors.

When I looked back, I noticed that the warriors on the left carried the unmistakable definition of White, while the warriors on the right were just as recognizable as Dark, though all their bodies were covered in indistinguishable white clay patterns, hidden by the night.

While the old man and I silently watched, the two lines converged, to meet at the top of the circle, directly across the fire from where I was.

They continued dancing, each line slowly moving into the other, until the two lines had merged and only one warrior could be seen at the head of the line. Then, slowly, from out of each side, the warriors moved until they were spread out in one long line, facing me now – and still dancing. And they all were dancing the same dance, together in unison.

The colors were now evenly distributed. Beside each Dark brother was a White brother, who was dancing beside a Dark brother, who was dancing beside a White brother … and so on down the line.

The dream began fading with the image of the line of brothers in alternating colors, still dancing …

I lay in the caravan in the darkness, the spear still firmly grasped in one hand, the red rock cupped in the other, waiting – and willing – for more. When nothing more arose, I reluctantly rolled over to go to sleep, wondering where the impetus for the vision had come from. As I drifted into sleep, the rounded rocky outcrop from under the line of hills appeared, and a grey mist was rising from it …

Chapter Seven

The Rain Rock

On the creek flats, hidden by the tall grass, is a large rock. It stands waist high, and takes the shape of an egg lying on its side, half-buried in the ground. This black mottled rock sits on a nexus of energy lines and, one day as I walked past, it called.

I strode in through the grasses and stood beside it, facing east towards the front of the land. Reaching out, I gently placed a hand upon it, feeling its rough texture beneath my fingers. Slowly, and respectfully, I stepped up onto it, moving towards the high point at the back. Here I could comfortably sit and tuck my feet under me.

Stillness surrounded me as I sat down cross-legged. With the sensations of the valley washing serenely over me, I looked across the open field where the faintest of breezes rustled the tops of the whitish grasses. My eyes drifted down to the darkness under the trees on the creek bank, and then up to the line of hills that rolled along the horizon line.

Overhead hung a blanket of low, dark clouds. This grey patchwork of clouds was slowly moving sideways across the sky, dampening the light and hushing the bush. Yet underlying the hum of the land was a thread of quiet expectancy and anticipation. As my gaze drifted back down, I noticed a small gum tree growing right in front of where I was sitting.

This tree intrigued me. It seemed to have popped out of the ground not long ago, yet already was higher than my outstretched hand when standing on the rock. I had been slightly perturbed by its closeness to the rock, but could only assume that it was meant to be. Still, I was curious to discover any interplay of energies.

Beyond the little tree, and standing directly behind it on the creek bank, was a tall white gum. Photographs taken near this large sentinel tree had shown a blur. At first, I had assumed the film had been over-exposed, but when flicking through the photos one day, I realized that these pictures had been taken at different times and from different positions, yet all showed a similar discoloration near it. Later, I'd searched around the tree, trying to pin-point the place where the energy was. A small patch of low grass was growing there – a different height and a deeper green to the surrounding grasses.

It was exquisite sitting there on the rock. The thick grey clouds formed a low ceiling, muting the vibrations of the outside world, and the soft breeze seemed to float right through me. It was peaceful, and utterly still. Looking along the line of the two trees, I half-closed my eyes in meditation.

I was sliding into the space between worlds, slowly sinking through the layers of consciousness, when a drop of water landed on my arm. For a moment, curiosity overcame meditation, and I opened my eyes to see that the light had dimmed even more, the heavy clouds having grown darker and lower, yet I couldn't see any sign of rain falling.

Then, against the shadows of the trees, the tiniest flecks of rain were seen. They lingered in the air, floating and swaying, as if unwilling to touch the earth. Unfelt and barely visible, these tiny drops slowly gathered, thickening in the air until a fine misty haze was drifting over the bleached grasses of the creek flats.

With eyes open, still immersed in meditation, I sat perched on the rock, watching these flecks gently falling. Not a sound was heard. Neither thought nor birdcall broke the stillness.

The meditation deepened, and so did the rain. The drops became larger and more frequent. A light rain began to fall. I could feel the land opening up, the earlier sense of anticipation and expectancy giving way to a joyous welcome of the rains.

The rain grew heavier until it was falling in steady sheets, pattering onto the tall grasses around me. I noticed I wasn't feeling wet or chilled, and wondered if my senses had been suspended, for I could feel neither the rock beneath, nor the rain upon me. Glancing down, I saw that my legs – tucked up underneath – were dry, and so were my arms! It was only the outer corners of my shoulders that were getting wet. For the rain was falling straight out of the sky, pulled down as if by a great magnet, and my hat was taking the brunt of the rain, while I sat dry under its little halo of protection. It felt like sitting in a cocoon, gently suspended above the fields, protected against the elements.

Within the stillness, the meditation began to expand – the inner world flowing towards the outer, the outer blending with the inner, the differentiating line between the two fading until there was no difference between eyes open or closed. Each had merged with the other, becoming inseparable.

The joyous thread of welcome that had started to open with the rains grew stronger. It became a vibrating force, filling the gap between creek flats and clouds, connecting them together …

The meditation, the rain, and the connecting force all became inextricably linked together. The deeper I slipped through the layers of meditation, the heavier it rained, and the greater became the connection.

In that moment – within the framework of inseparable connection – an image, an idea, a concept arose.

The words, Determination, Regeneration, Growth appeared, echoing as the connection deepened.

And I was shown creation – of a rock/plant/animal – and the keen determination for that life to grow, to flourish, to continue. And how, as this life force expanded, it began to weave a web upon the fabric of nature, to reach out and touch the world – connecting, communicating, enhancing, and finally to gradually diminish and ebb back into the basic elements.

Growth. Regeneration. Determination.

Encapsulating one concept.

Where did these ideas originate? I saw them within myself, yet they were outside as well. I saw them within creation – yet they were also within the connection. But they did not appear to begin, nor solely exist, in either. It seemed impossible to determine their origin for they were like the softest zephyr gliding by, gently wafting within reach and then disappearing at the slightest gesture.

With it came the realization that co-creating occurs when the link between Humanity and Nature is pure, unrestrained. Perhaps, it is not so much a co-creating as a blending into Oneness – of Intent.

My beliefs in co-creating were going through a rapid change!

And within that connection, equally shared, the rain grew heavier and heavier until it thundered down, beating a loud staccato rhythm on the ground.

Chapter Eight

Feet on the Ground, Head in the Clouds

A ball of blue and green appeared
Hanging against a midnight sky
Overlaid with wisps of white

It was the earth
Looking pretty and delicate
In the far distance

A phantom figure arose
Huge – towering above the earth
Caped in shining white

My perception drew closer
The earth colors grew brighter
The figure loomed larger

Until I was standing within his shadow
Encompassed by his glow
And gazing down upon the world

White wings appeared
From between his shoulder blades
Inching out into space

Feet on the Ground, Head in the Clouds

My point of perception moved
To stand beside his shoulder
And look down upon the emerging wings

Thin strands of white
Cross-weaved by four
Were they composed

Growing finer as they extended
Deeper and deeper into space
Able to stretch to infinity, it seemed

Unmoved stood the figure above the earth
The threads dancing and weaving
Flowing out within the wings

Until they became a river
Than twisted and turned and spun
Joyous in its tide

Far out in space
The wingtips began to curl
And point towards the earth

The arms of the phantom
Still flowing, still growing
Swung round in great arcs

The tips reached out to the planet
Slowing as they neared
To disappear behind

All was still.
Nestled within the phantom's shadow
I watched as …

A band of light rose up from behind the earth
And swept down below
Vibrant against the night sky

For the wingtips had joined
To become a single thread of white
That quickly expanded out.

The phantom rushed to meet it
His body billowing out
Arcing towards the spreading wing

Above and below black poles closed over
As the phantom and wings met
And the world was encased in a sphere of light

The sphere started shrinking
My perception moved nearer
Closer and closer until …

The world transformed
Into a series of white lines
That moved into my heart

The phantom and my perception merged
And together we lay ourselves upon the earth
Tenderly hugging her

And we were dissolved in Light
Beating with the heart of the earth
As Three became One.

Chapter Nine

The Afghan Shaman

Clockwise earth spin – puts the energy out from the earth heart. Counter brings in energy from the universes. Together – the earth and universes pause – shifting.

NTA

The Shift
14 September 2001

Meditation came, after midnight.
Tired. Waiting, watching.
A vision arose …

Two circles. Dancing around a brightly glowing pile.
All dressed in white, holding hands.
A happy, carefree dance.

A circle within a circle.
The center of the ruins.
Each circle spinning in different directions.

Men and women – different clothes, many styles,
Smiling, dancing, circling together.
Beautiful.

"Ah," one man beckoned, his arm lifted high,
An invitation to join.
"Come! You can't resist," his smile seemed to say.
And it was irresistible!

(His eyes held a knowing.
A look that said, "Come, friend," as if he knew me well.
Perhaps he did. Still, time to play.)

Joined hands with the circle of white.
It moved with a joyous abandonment.
There was no lingering regret or sorrow.

A lady laughed from across the circle.
Kicking her legs high, and smiling at me as she glided round,
Hand in hand with her partners.

Contagious,
Was her carefreeness.
All doubts were dispelled.

Smiling sheepishly, I began to move.
I jerked. I tried to flow.
They laughed, urging me on.

The Knowing One held high his arm,
A partner's hand in his grasp,
A gesture of exuberance, encouraging me.

Lifting my arms, I danced, still feeling awkward.
Yet they laughed all the more, and went back to their dancing.
Hand in hand, kicking and swinging, round and round the circle.
Happy, carefree, joyous abandonment.

Spirals in the Sand

While holidaying at my parent's place, I had an irrepressible urge one evening to drive down to the beach.

A familiar ocean breeze gusted through the deserted car park, and I sat in the car listening to the waves washing on to the rocks below. The night air blowing in through the car window was warm and thick, scented with childhood memories. I wanted space tonight, a sense of privacy, yet I was expecting to find late night holiday-makers around, so I was surprised when the picnic area was empty.

I wandered down past the picnic tables towards the beach. The night gathered around me as the glow of the streetlight was left behind, and I slowed, placing my feet in the dark. At the edge of the grass, I slipped off my sandals and stepped onto the beach, happily wriggling my toes in the cool smooth sand, while the sea breeze gently caressed the hairs on my bare arms and legs. There was a sense of exhilaration, of building excitement. I wanted to walk, or even run, along the beach in the dark, to release this energy in a burst of exuberant activity.

The logical mind appeared. "Something might be in the sand," it worried, "looking for unwary toes." Concerned, I peered down at my feet, surprised to be able to see them in the dark. Not well perhaps, but I could dimly see my feet and legs and the area of sand around me. I looked behind me. The streetlight was too far away to throw any light down here, and there was no moon overhead. Shrugging it aside, I stood enjoying the oceanic night air.

Voices called out. There were revelers somewhere on the beach and, although I couldn't see them, I could hear them laughing, splashing and shouting out in the dark. The sound of the people added an impetus, a sense of nervous energy to the evening.

My head began to move from side to side, my eyes scanning the beach. The body was drawn further onto the sands. I walked slowly forward, peering down, head swaying. An area drew me, unmarked on the beach, midway between the grass and the basalt rocks along the water's edge. My head stopped its swaying motion, as my eyes focused on a spot on the sand. Standing silently above it, I bent over and piled the sand into a little cushion, and sat down upon it with my legs crossed.

After a few moments of sitting quietly in the dark, I reached down and, putting a finger in the sand, slowly drew a circle around myself. I sat up and softly offered a prayer to the spirits. Then, without conscious volition, the left hand moved forward and began to make a circular motion on the sand.

Strangely detached, I watched the palm rubbing the sand in a clockwise direction, round and round. The feel of the fine white sand was smooth and slippery beneath the heel of my palm. Then the other hand reached forward and, it too, began to make circular motions, but in the opposite direction. Round indentations began to form in the sand under the heel of my palms.

I stopped to examine what was happening, to bring the conscious mind forward, to analyze what was going on. With difficulty, I broke the connection and looked quizzically down at the two handmade spirals in the sand when I realized, with a jolt of alarm, that I couldn't remember which way my hands had been turning! Quickly, I leaned over and gently placed my palms in the center of the spirals.

Concentrating deeply, I slowly started moving them around in, what I hoped was, the original directions. But it didn't feel right. I stopped and reversed the directions. Still it didn't flow. I reversed directions again and finally, in desperation, moved my hands together in the same direction.

Nothing worked; my mind had gone blank. It was as if the brain was confused and couldn't co-ordinate the right and left hands. I paused, letting my mind drift, listening to the waves washing onto the rocks, unseen in the night, and feeling the salty wind on my face. Leaning forward, I placed my hands in the spirals, and watched my hands begin to move again.

As I sat there making spirals in the sand, it slowly dawned on me that I could see my hands in the dark. Looking down, I could see my legs as well! I was sitting in a small pool of light surrounded by the night. I wondered if car headlights or visitors were somehow intruding, but apart from the distant streetlight at the picnic tables, the night was dark. Bemused, yet somehow unconcerned, I turned back to the spirals.

After a time my hands began to slow, and finally to stop. Gently, I lifted my palms off the sands and saw sparkles of light spinning around the imprinted lines left by my hands. I watched, mesmerized, as the tiny sparkles traveled the lines, twisting and flashing in the direction of each spiraled print. Yet something else was needed. Reaching forward, I lightly dipped a fingertip in the sand and drew a symbol between the two spirals … and then added another symbol.

I leaned back onto the little cushion of sand. The pressures were relaxed from my mind leaving only the sensations of the warm moist evening around me: the fresh salty breeze tugging at my hair and clothes, the sound of the waves, and the silken feel of cool smooth sand beneath.

As I gazed peacefully around, I noticed that the light had grown bigger. It was now extending out past the circle in the sand. Curiously, I stood up and brushed the fine sand off. The light was slowly, but steadily, moving out in all directions, pushing back the darkness. The circle grew until it reached the edge of the black basalt rocks that lined the shore, and behind me to where it just touched the edge of the grass – a radius of about a dozen paces.

It was clear as daylight within the circle; everything stood out in amazing detail on the beach. Yet there seemed no discernible source for it. I looked up, half-expecting a light in the sky to be beaming down, but the night was dark. Even the stars seemed dimmed and remote in the thick, heavy air. Was it radiating from the center, I wondered? Cautiously, I took a few steps within the circle. The light didn't change. It seemed to be coming from everywhere at once.

As I stood there, looking about the sands and into the darkness beyond, I wondered about the reason behind this event. Imagination lent ideas to another time, another body, when this ritual would have been performed knowingly. I tried to sense some energetic connection with that time. There appeared the image of an aboriginal face faintly before me, and I thought I may have heard words, but everything was vague …

Unsure what to do next, I waited. The clear light shone steadily, neither growing bigger nor shrinking.

I heard a noise and turned hastily around. There was no-one there, but it lent a hurried urgency to the experience, and I wondered if I could be seen here in the dark, and if the circle of light was visible as well.

After a while, when nothing more happened, I felt it was time to leave. I smoothed the sand cushion over, regretfully breaking the circle, and slowly wandered back onto the lawn. Sliding my sandy feet back into my sandals, I walked up the slope past the picnic tables to the car park. At the top, I looked back. The circle of light was still visible, shining gently on the beach. As I watched, it gradually dimmed, until only the faintest glow remained.

The Afghan Shaman

A voice called my name, pulling me up into consciousness from the twilight realm between sleeping and waking. I lay there half-asleep, certain I'd heard a voice. The night was very still and quiet.

I was drifting back into sleep when the voice called a second time. It was very clear – a distinct call. I lay there, listening and waiting – and wondering.

I had begun to drift off again when the voice called a third time. Puzzled, and now awake, I climbed up on to my elbows and turned in the direction of the voice.

It seemed to be coming from above and behind my head – from a point beyond the bedroom wall!

I lay back pondering, looking for rational explanations, and waiting for inspiration. Nothing arose. Unsure what else to do, I mentally turned towards this point from where the voice had come.

As soon as I turned my attention in that direction, the mind became extraordinarily focused, the energy flowing upwards, all thoughts being drawn to a single spot in my forehead.

Waves of light began streaming across my inner vision. Like an observer, I watched as these waves became circles of golden energy, starting from outside my vision and contracting in, to meet and merge with this spot in the center of my forehead. Wave after wave flowed in. The contracting circles transformed into a grid. A pattern of vibrating yellow lines were radiating out from the center, connecting the incoming waves together.

A white line started spiraling from out of this place above and behind my head, growing larger as it neared. It became a spinning funnel, racing toward me with incredible speed, its swirling white walls streaked with grey. Then it opened above my head, and with a sense of vertigo, I was sucked backwards into its maw.

I was speeding down a darkened tunnel, spinning and twisting, and then an opening appeared and, with a rush, I was thrust out into brilliant sunlight.

I stood momentarily blinded, the light harsh on my eyes. Slowly the brightness dimmed and the scene took on clarity. A desert lay before me. A flat wasteland stretched away into the distance, the shimmering sands only occasionally broken by a rock or shrub, to purple mountains looking tiny on the horizon.

"Where is this place?" I wondered. "Was this somewhere in Australia? Or on another continent? Was it another place – or time – altogether?"

As the clarity increased, I found myself squatting on a smooth red rock that towered back behind me in a cliff face. Below me passed small groups of people, struggling along a dirt road across the foreground of this desert scene. All were heavily dressed against the climate, and determination and haste were evident in their movements. They seemed to be fleeing, yet I could sense no enemy on the horizon. Then the thought arose that they were leaving before the storm broke.

A group stopped on the road not far from me. Two men in front, heavily burdened, were called to a halt. Their impatient movements suggested a desire to continue quickly. Behind them walked a lady and two young children. To my right, and further back, I saw a figure approaching.

A younger man, wearing white, walked up and stopped just below me. He began untying a thick white sheath bound with cord. I peered down from my vantage point to see what he was doing. Seemingly unaware of my presence, he extracted from the sheath a small pouch, tied at the neck with a drawstring. Loosening the drawstring, he opened the bag and, without looking up to where I squatted above his head, held the mouth open for me to look inside.

I leaned over inquisitively yet, aware that these were his personal possessions, didn't want to intrude. I felt a reassurance, a calming touch, and cautiously looked down into the bag. The bright sunlight threw the inside of the pouch into black shadow. I couldn't see anything. I tried altering my vision, straining to perceive what he wanted me to see. I withdrew my gaze, frustrated. The shaman waited patiently in front of me. I tried again.

The vision changed. I could see inside the bag. The sides were made of reddish-brown leather, and scattered across the bottom were various items – a green gem, a small bone, a dark red rock, and other items I can't remember clearly. Each item sat by itself in its own space on the bottom, not touching any of the other items. Again, aware that they were his personal objects, I was hesitant in impressing my thoughts upon them, in placing any energetic overlays on their composition, yet felt his encouragement. I studied the items, wondering how he came by them, and for what purposes he used them. Although the items bore his personal signature, they didn't reveal their natures to me.

At one point, the woman left the group waiting nearby and came over. Placing a hand on his arm, she spoke to him. I intuited that this was his wife, and was asking if they were to leave soon. He gently replied and she moved away, and then he turned back to me. I don't think she saw me there.

From my position on the rock, head bowed, peering down, I watched him reach into the pouch. He wriggled his fingers down through the small opening until he'd finally managed to squeeze his entire hand into the little bag. His fingers began moving around inside like he was looking for something; I could see the outlines of his fingers against the sides. He seemed to be taking a long time doing it …

Then he started to swing the pouch round and round in circles. Baffled by this, I was closely following his movements, when I saw the bag was higher up on his wrist than before. Wondering how he could have forced his hand even further into that small leather pouch, I widened my gaze, to see that his hand had disappeared through the bottom of the bag! Startled, I stared where his hand should've been. It looked like he had pushed his hand down into nothingness!

As I intently watched, bewildered by what I saw, a light began to glimmer from the middle of the bag. It grew more intense. A star formed; rays of many colors were emanating from it.

And then out of the star, a red ring appeared, hovering in the air. A green ring appeared next, sitting beneath the red ring. And then more followed, until a line of glowing rings, each a different color, hovered before the bag. The star in the center of the bag shone more brightly, capturing my attention, and suddenly I was falling into the Light to see …

Part Three

The shaman, sitting cross-legged in space, and dressed in glowing white. In front of him was the world, the size of a large ball, the greens and blues of the earth unmistakable. In his hand was a short thick length of rope – camel hair came to mind. He held it up so that the rope dangled above the world, and then slowly he lowered it until the frayed end had disappeared into the top of the earth. He lowered it even further and I watched, absorbed in the vision, as his hand neared the top of the world. He stopped and slowly lifted the rope up. And then he lowered it, to dip the rope into the earth again and again. Aware of my intense scrutiny, he looked up and smiled.

This final image of the Afghan Shaman dipping the rope into the world still arises, and I often wonder about it. What was it he was trying to show me? What is it I am to understand? Yet, somewhere on the periphery of my mind, lies the image of the world turning into a shimmering series of white lines …

Acknowledgements

With Respect and Gratitude to …

Brett J. (Mira'ji) – for Help and Support.

NTA – for Love and Understanding.

Stacey and Dave – for Comments and Suggestions.

Renee Meuller – for Copyright Permission.

Graham – for the Snake Border and Knot.

Magicheart – for his poem 'The Ghost People'.

To those who participated in the stories,

And to those who read them.

The stories continue in …

Diary of a JOURNEYMAN

Book Two in the Series
Diaries of a Shaman

www.shamandiary.com